CW01459466

MINI
MADRID

ROUGH GUIDES

YOUR TAILOR-MADE TRIP
STARTS HERE

Tailor-made trips and unique adventures crafted by local experts

HOW ROUGHGUIDES.COM/TRIPS WORKS

STEP 1
Pick your dream destination, tell us what you want and submit an enquiry.

STEP 2
Fill in a short form to tell your local expert about you dream trip and preference

STEP 3
Our local expert will craft your tailor-made itinerary. You'll be able to tweak and refine it until you're completely satisfied.

STEP 4
Book online with ease, pa your bags and enjoy the trip! Our local expert will b on hand 24/7 while you're on the road.

PLAN AND BOOK YOUR TRIP AT
ROUGHGUIDES.COM/TRIPS

How to download your Free eBook

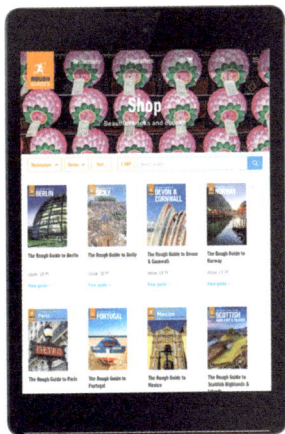

1. Visit **www.roughguides.com/free-ebook** or scan the **QR code** opposite

2. Enter the code **madrid918**

3. Follow the simple step-by-step instructions

For troubleshooting contact: mail@roughguides.com

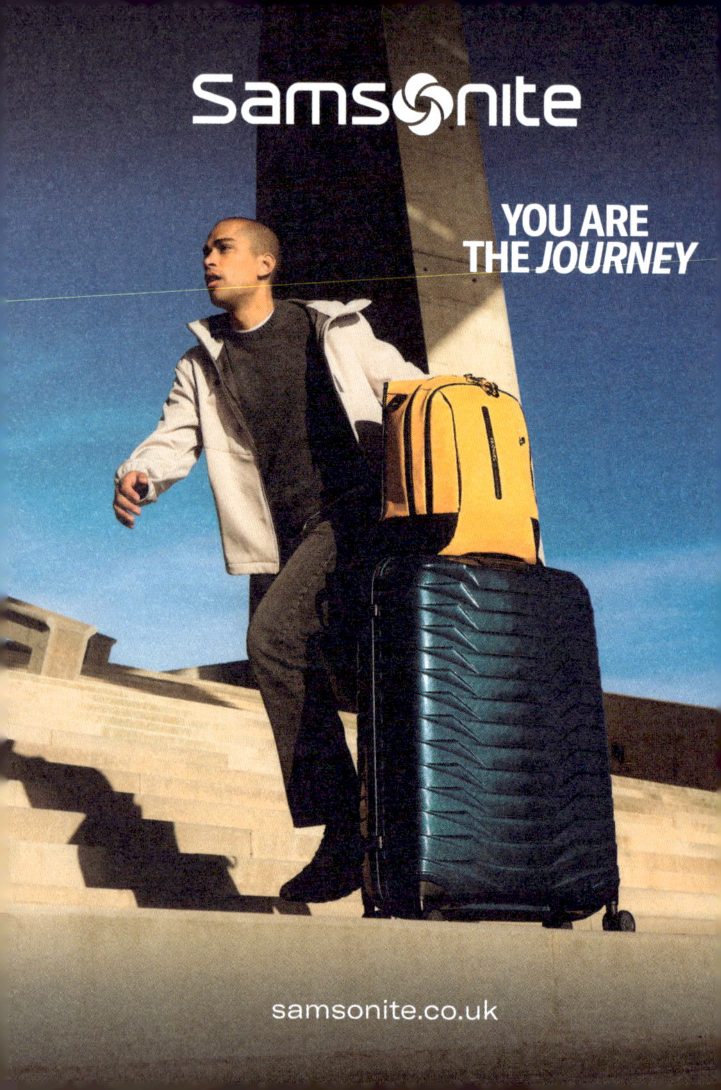
Samsonite
YOU ARE
THE JOURNEY
samsonite.co.uk

Contents

Introduction

Madrid was little more than a farming town on the arid central plains of Castile when Felipe II plucked it from his royal cap in 1561 and proclaimed it home to the Spanish Court. Ever since then Madrid, which took the reins of Spain's Golden Age, hasn't stopped growing and asserting itself. Though one of Europe's youngest capitals, it's had both the time and the ambition to rival Spain's more historic cities, including Seville and Valencia. Today it is Spain's political and economic hub. Only Barcelona matches its metropolitan importance.

The heart of Spain

Behind Felipe II's royal decree lay a clear logic: Madrid, smack in the centre of Iberia, would promote the monarchy's authority over regional power bases in a newly unified Spain. Today, Madrid *is* that cohesive centre, and more besides. It is a city to which people have migrated from all over Spain in search of new opportunities, a place where few people claim deep roots.

Yet at the centre of the modern metropolis, a region of just over six million people, its medieval heart lies almost untouched, the alleyways often eerily silent at night. For while Spain has leaped forward economically since the 1970s, Madrid is no less characteristically Iberian for that and revels in its traditional way of life. Once, its immigrants were from the Spanish countryside. Today, its newcomers more often come from Latin America and Eastern Europe, but their new customs and

> **NOTES**
>
> 'De Madrid al cielo' is a popular saying, which means 'From Madrid, one step to heaven.' As western Europe's highest capital (around 650m above sea level), Madrid boasts spectacular sierra skies and autumn sunsets, captured by Velázquez in his paintings.

fiestas are equally absorbed into the local pattern of life.

Other regions of Spain, such as Catalonia and the Basque Country, are more proudly independent in their traditions. Barcelona, Granada and older Castilian court cities possess greater architecture, and many smaller Spanish cities have finer historic quarters, but *madrileños* don't begrudge those places anything. Their city may be a planned bureaucrat's town, but its buzzing quality of life keeps Madrid just one rung down from heaven, or so the local saying goes – and many *madrileños* believe it.

Taking a break in Plaza Mayor

Culture and nightlife

In recent years the city has nurtured Spain's most sophisticated cultural life: opera, theatre, *zarzuela* (a form of light comic opera), contemporary dance, jazz and rock, film, circus and graffiti. All have found new audiences here, as has flamenco, Spain's most unique art form.

Nevertheless, Madrid's single greatest cultural draw remains its cluster of superb art museums. On the grand Paseo del Prado are three of Europe's finest: the world-class Museo Nacional del Prado, the Museo Thyssen-Bornemisza and the Museo Nacional Centro de Arte Reina Sofía, the latter home to Pablo Picasso's monumental painting, *Guernica*. Madrid's collection of Spanish

Old Masters – Velázquez, El Greco, Goya, Zurbarán and more – is unrivalled.

Gregarious at heart, *madrileños* are night creatures, hopping in and out of *tabernas* (cave-like taverns), restaurants and bars for tapas, Spanish wine and animated conversation until the early hours. The *movida* of the early 1980s, a spontaneous burst of creative nightlife, has given Madrid a reputation it works hard to maintain. Nightlife still starts and goes on late – very late.

Geography

In terms of scale, Madrid's city centre hardly feels like that of a major capital city, and it is easily covered on foot. The city's heart

The nineteenth-century Palacio de Cristal in Retiro Park

WHAT'S NEW

Plaza de España (see page 74): A major revamp of this park-like space has seen roads thrust underground and pedestrians prioritized – the new plaza connects no fewer than eight major parts of the city, enabling locals and visitors alike to reach the Palacio Real (see page 39), the Almudena Cathedral (see page 41) and the Templo de Debod (see page 75) without so much as crossing the road.

Puerta del Sol (see page 44): Major renovations of one of Madrid's most iconic squares have also now been completed, making Puerta del Sol and its environs more attractive, more pedestrian-friendly and more accessible.

Palacio del Capricho Museum: By the time you read this, a brand new museum should be up and running, set in a hitherto abandoned palace in the Barajas district.

Palacio de Cristal (see page 62): The iconic "Glass Palace" in Retiro Park (see page 61) should also have opened, after refurbishment, by the time you read this.

is Old (or Habsburg) Madrid, a largely sixteenth-century city built around the narrow, winding streets of an earlier Muslim settlement. Its centrepiece is the splendid porticoed Plaza Mayor, rebuilt three times after fires. Nearby are glimpses of the Arab walls, medieval plazas, monasteries and the Palacio Real (Royal Palace), built on the site of the older Muslim Alcázar. The lively Puerta del Sol, still the beating heart of the city, marks the eastern edge of Habsburg Madrid.

The Bourbon monarchs of the eighteenth century fostered the city's expansion further east. They commissioned grand avenues and boulevards, in addition to fountains and gateways. Bourbon Madrid is best symbolized by the handsome Paseo del Prado, named a UNESCO World Heritage Site in 2021, and the banking mansions leading from here towards the Puerta del Sol. Wedged between this monumental part of town and the historic old town are the city's most characterful popular quarters, such as Lavapiés, Chueca and Malasaña.

Modern Madrid grew unrelentingly in all directions from the early nineteenth century. Uptown Salamanca is an elegant if faded quarter of apartment buildings and sophisticated shops built around a grid of streets bordered by La Castellana and Paseo de Recoletos, the northward extensions of the Prado boulevard. Both are lined with pavement cafés. Since the 1980s, La Castellana has pushed further north, beyond the financial district. Its northern limit is now marked by Las Cuatro Torres, four spectacular architect-designed towers.

Architecture

Madrid's diverse architecture traces the prevailing styles of the different eras in which it spread outwards. Moving from the centre, one passes from stately sixteenth-century buildings with wrought-iron balconies, brick facades and stone features, to baroque Bourbon palaces, neoclassical buildings and the elegant belle époque, Art Nouveau and Art Deco styles of the Gran Vía. The severe architecture of Franco's dictatorship, on La Castellana, gave way during the 1990s to a wave of eye-catching flagship architecture and, just as important, restoration of the popular old quarters. Their quiet, colourful, tree-lined streets are now just as beautiful as the city's grander areas.

THE CASTIZO SPIRIT

Madrid's flea market, the Rastro, is the mecca of *castizo* culture. Like London's Cockney culture, it is famed for its quick and witty wordplay and its strong community spirit. *Castizo* culture dates back to the eighteenth century, when the ruling classes began to adopt French styles, and in response the local people developed a swaggering chutzpah and an exaggerated accent deliberately incomprehensible to an outsider.

Modernity and tradition

Madrid was at the forefront of the dynamic Spain that emerged after Franco's death in 1975, which brought an end to forty years of dictatorship and cultural and intellectual isolation. Once unshakeably conservative and Catholic, Spain today has one of Europe's lowest birth rates, rapidly falling church attendance, and legally recognized gay marriage. Twenty-five years of economic boom have been followed by prolonged economic crisis, during which time *madrileños* have been rethinking their city's future.

Cuatro Torres skyscrapers

What has endured throughout a century of political upheaval and transitions is the love of exuberant street life. After work, *madrileños* spill onto pavements and pack outdoor cafés, those of all ages still take the evening *paseo*, while pensioners play cards or chess in the parks. Come evening, people crowd into the city's bars.

Madrid clings to *castizo* (working-class *madrileño*) traditions too. Las Ventas bullring is a shrine for aficionados of bullfighting (*la corrida*) while local *fiestas* such as San Isidro, a celebration of the city's patron saint, are affectionately enjoyed.

'*Nueve meses de invierno y tres de infierno…*' ('Nine months of winter and three of hell…'): the shifts between freezing winters and scorching summers, elegant boulevards and characterful backstreets

WHEN TO GO

Spain's high central plains, which include Madrid, suffer from fierce extremes of temperature – stiflingly hot in summer (late June through to the end of August), and swept by bitterly freezing winds, and the odd sprinkling of snow, in winter (December to February). The shoulder periods of winter and autumn are pretty long, though, and these make for the optimum times to visit – you're likely to experience ideal temperatures, low humidity and some of the brightest sunshine in Europe. August is the country's own holiday month – while the costas are at their most crowded, Madrid can be pretty sleepy during this period, since everyone who can leaves for their annual break, and many restaurants and sites of interest close completely.

are marked yet easy ones. There are other contrasts too: Madrid remains a city of *barrios*, or quarters, each of which revels in its own individuality. Traditions are as celebrated as contemporary arts, and it is this kaleidoscopic mix that makes the city such a memorable place.

Options outside Madrid

Madrid is the perfect base for exploring Castile. A trio of UNESCO-honoured cities lie within an hour's journey. Toledo, Spain's former capital, set on a mound above a river moat, keeps an outstanding architectural legacy from its Christian, Jewish and Muslim medieval culture. Segovia, once a royal stronghold, has a fairy-tale castle, a 2,000-year-old Roman aqueduct and wonderful Romanesque churches. The city of Ávila, the birthplace of St Teresa, may be viewed from its perfectly preserved medieval city wall.

Closer to Madrid is the royal monastery of El Escorial, a mausoleum and palace built by Felipe II, from which he governed the Spanish empire. Aranjuez and Chinchón, to the south of Madrid, may be visited together in a day by car. One is an ornamental royal palace and the other a pleasant Castilian country town.

Rooftop bar at the Círculo de Bellas Artes

SUSTAINABLE TRAVEL

It's more than a little worrying for tourists to Spain that one of the most prominent sustainability issues here of late has been, well, tourism.

While Madrid has avoided the largest of the 'tourists go home' protests (which first erupted in the Canary Islands in 2024, and spread to Barcelona, the Valencian coast, parts of Andalucía, even in areas along the northern coast, and more), and will never receive a cruise ship, as the national capital, the issue remains pertinent here. The anger tends to revolve around locals being priced out of their own home cities or areas – by staying at licensed accommodation, rather than using Airbnb and the like, you can avoid making a larger-than-necessary footprint on the local housing market.

10 Things not to miss

1 PLAZA MAYOR
Take a seat at a terrace café and watch the world go by at the busy centre of local social life. See page 34.

2 MUSEO NACIONAL CENTRO DE ARTE REINA SOFÍA
A popular showcase of art of the twentieth and twenty-first centuries, including work by Picasso and Luis Buñuel. See page 59.

3 PUERTA DEL SOL
The plaza's clock tower overlooks the bustling heart of Madrid and chimes in Spain's New Year revelry. See page 44.

4 EL ESCORIAL
The palace created by Felipe II, where Spain's Golden Age is writ large. See page 79.

5 THE PRADO
Spain's rich artistic heritage is conserved in one of the world's most prestigious museums. See page 50.

6 MONASTERIO DE LAS DESCALZAS REALES
A unique chance to see the artistic heritage of a working convent over 450 years. See page 43.

7 PLAZA SANTA ANA
A great place to start *el tapeo*, the 'tapas crawl'. See page 45.

8 PALACIO REAL
Elegant centre of royal Madrid. See page 39.

9 LA ERMITA DE SAN ANTONIO DE LA FLORIDA
Goya's frescoes adorn the cupola of this eighteenth-century chapel. See page 77.

10 PARQUE DEL BUEN RETIRO
Its trees, lawns and lake make this Madrid's most child-friendly green space. See page 61.

A perfect day in Madrid

9AM

Santa Ana. Join locals for coffee and fried *churros* on this tree-lined plaza in this charming eighteenth-century quarter. Don't miss the colourful tiled friezes on bars around the square.

10AM

Green oasis. Explore the beautifully tended Real Jardín Botánico where dahlias were first planted in Europe.

11AM

The Prado. One of the world's greatest art galleries. Do not miss the restored Renaissance Patio de los Jerónimos. The Spanish paintings include masterworks by Diego Velázquez and Francisco de Goya.

1PM

Art and aperitivos. Take a break in the top floor café of Herzog de Meuron's CaixaForum arts centre, where you can sip an *aperitivo* and look down on the adjacent vertical garden – a rich tapestry of globally sourced plant varieties.

2PM

Classic cocido madrileño. Madrid's celebrated chickpea stew is cooked the old-fashioned way – in earthenware pots, over charcoal – at *La Bola*, where you lunch with locals.

4PM

Guernica. Pablo Picasso conceived *Guernica*, as a protest against the Nazi bombing of the eponymous Basque village, in 1937. See it hanging alongside his preparatory drawings at the Museo Nacional Centro de Arte Reina Sofía.

5.30PM

Shop till you drop. Pedestrianized Calle de Fuencarral, running off Gran Vía, is the city's most fashionable shopping drag. Here you can find hip Spanish fashion brands from Camper shoes to Custo and Hoss Intropia clothes, plus other European fashion.

7.30PM

Tapas time. Enjoy the city's magical dusk light with an evening stroll through the sloping old streets that link the Plaza Mayor to the Cava Baja in the medieval old town. Locals end the day there with a glass of fine wine and tapas.

10.30PM

Flamenco. Book ahead for the late show at one of the city's *tablaos*, or flamenco clubs, like *Casa Patas*. Here you will see artists perform flamenco song, guitar and dance in an intimate and atmospheric environment.

LATE

Churros...again? It's a Madrileño custom to finish off a late night with *churros* and chocolate (don't laugh... it's healthier than a British kebab), meaning that it's possible to end the day exactly how you started it.

Madrid for foodies

9AM

Churros in a local institution. Join locals for chocolate and *churros* at *San Ginés* (see page 112), a round-the-clock institution serving much the same since 1894.

11AM

Brunch by the palace. Before or after a visit to the Palacio Real (see page 39), pop into the *Café de Oriente* (see page 120) while it's not busy for coffee or brunch in opulent surrounds.

2PM

Hunt down a Michelin-star meal. For lunch, those who've made advance bookings can hunt down the offerings of one of Spain's many top chefs, such as the two Michelin-starred *Paco Roncero Restaurante* (see page 121), Dani García's *Smoked Room* and *Tragabuches*, or Dabiz Muñoz's *DiverXO* (see page 122). Why lunch over dinner? Lunch can often be a bargain in Spain, even at lauded venues.

5PM

Arty coffee. Pop into *Café Gijón* (see page 121) for coffee, tea, juice or snacks at this old literary café, after visiting the Prado – or before visiting, if you'd like to take advantage of its free-entry window.

8PM

The world's oldest restaurant. For dinner, give *Botín* (see page 118) a go – once listed in the *Guinness Book of Records* as the world's oldest continuously-running restaurant, it's great for Castilian dishes such as *sopa de ajo* (see page 111) and grilled meats.

10PM

Tapas time. Spaniards tend to forget about dinner until late. Join them in the medieval old town (see page 34), drinking fine wine and eating tapas (see box, page 115) in old coaching inns; it's customary to have a drink while sharing a *ración* or *tapa*, then repeat the trick elsewhere ad nauseam.

Madrid on a budget

8AM

Pan con tomate. Wherever you're staying in Madrid – nay, in Spain – you won't be far from a restaurant, café or bar serving the local breakfast favourite: tomato on toast, usually with coffee on the side, for a bargain price. For a little extra you can have *jamón ibérico* (a slice of cured ham) on top, and/or a freshly squeezed orange juice.

10AM

Free local history. Learn about Madrid for free at the excellent Museo de San Isidro (see page 37).

12PM

Go local for lunch. Top up on a budget with the locals' favourite snack food – *bocatas de calamares* (squid sandwiches), available all over town.

1PM

Wednesday art bonus. If you're around on a Wednesday or during national holidays, you can get into the Real Academia de Bellas Artes de San Fernando (see page 48) for free, to see

works by Goya, Velázquez, Murillo and Rubens.

3PM

A walk in the park. Go for a stroll around the Retiro Park (see page 61), a verdant park that provides some great photo opportunities. At weekends, there are puppet shows by the Puerta de Alcalá, and often South American musicians performing by the lake.

6–9PM

The world's greatest art, for free. There's free entry during the last couple of opening hours at the Prado (see page 50) and Reina Sofía (see page 59) galleries; the latter is usually open an hour later, and both are not too far from each other, so if pressed for time, and with clear targets, you could actually do both this way.

9.30PM

100 Montaditos. Beloved by students, this pan-national chain is a Spanish institution, and a penny-pincher's dream – you can fill up and have a few drinks without breaching the ten-euro barrier.

History

Though prehistoric remains from the Palaeolithic, Neolithic and Bronze Ages have been unearthed in the Manzanares valley, Madrid was just a quiet farming town before its sudden elevation to capital city in 1561.

Over many centuries Madrid's future significance would have been hard to foresee. The Romans dominated and settled large parts of the Iberian peninsula, but left nothing of consequence here. Muslim armies invaded the peninsula in AD 711 via North Africa and overran most of what is Spain today within a decade. It is clear from the Arabic origin of Madrid's name – 'place of many springs', variously recorded

Fernando and Isabel greet Christopher Columbus

as Magerit, Mayrit or Magrit – that their appreciation of its endless supply of snow and spring water underlay the growth of the early town.

During three and a half centuries of Muslim rule, the local army built a full-scale fortified palace or *alcázar* on the west-facing heights of Madrid commanding the Manzanares valley.

NOTES

Mudéjar architecture refers to a style made popular after the Christian reconquest of Spain. Christians employed Muslim craftsmen to construct buildings with intricate carved and painted Moorish decoration.

After several unsuccessful skirmishes, the Christian forces of Alfonso VI captured Madrid in 1083, and the *alcázar* became a fort of the crown of Castile. During a counter-offensive in 1109, the town was overrun by Muslims, but the Christianized fortress held and Madrid became a secure walled Christian town. Nonetheless, the Muslim community and later its lifestyle continued to be an everyday part of life here long after the fall of Granada in 1492.

Meanwhile, Madrid enjoyed brief prominence in 1309 when Ferdinand IV and his Cortes, an early version of parliament, held a formal meeting in the fledgling town.

Fernando and Isabel, the Catholic monarchs whose marriage united the kingdoms of Aragon and Castile, first visited Madrid in 1477. They appreciated the town's loyalty, but cultured Toledo continued secure in its role as Spain's capital.

Spain's Golden Age

Under Fernando and Isabel, Spain underwent a dramatic transformation. In 1492 the couple presided over the conquest and discovery of the New World. Over the following century it was to bring great wealth to Spain from the newly established American colonies. Often called the country's Golden Age, this was a century of Spanish political supremacy, accompanied by marvels of art and literature,

NOTES

Felipe II ignored the advice of his father, Carlos I: 'If you wish to conserve your dominions,' he counselled, 'leave the court in Toledo; if you wish to increase them move it to Lisbon; if you do not mind losing them, take it to Madrid.'

although the roots of decline were present in tensions with the converted Jews and Muslims, economic inflation, and the Inquisition's censorship of cultural life.

Fernando and Isabel were consummate Spaniards, committed to the expansion of the crown, closely controlled from an itinerant court. By contrast, their grandson, who assumed the throne as Carlos I in 1516, was born in Flanders in 1500 and could barely express himself in Spanish. The first of the Habsburg dynasty, he packed his retinue with Burgundian and Flemish nobles.

Soon after his arrival in Spain, he inherited the title of Holy Roman Emperor, as Carlos V. His responsibilities in northern Europe kept him busy, away from the royal residences of Toledo, Segovia, Valladolid and Madrid. While the monarch was away, revolts broke out in a number of Spanish cities, including Madrid, where the rebels occupied the *alcázar* (by then a royal palace). The insurrection was quashed and its leaders executed, but the king got the message: he desperately needed to pay more attention to his Spanish subjects.

Madrid's rise to Capital

In 1556, Carlos abdicated in favour of his son, Felipe II – good news for Spain, and even better for Madrid. Felipe moved the royal court here from Toledo in 1561, converting a town of fewer than fifteen thousand people into the capital of the world's greatest empire. Madrid expanded in a largely improvised way, increasing nearly eight-fold in population in just fifty years. Spain's fortunes as a whole were more volatile. Felipe II took credit for a rousing naval victory at Lepanto against the Turks, but less than two decades later Spain was subjected to the humiliating defeat of its 'invincible' armada, at the hands of Sir Francis Drake. Felipe II's greatest architectural legacy was El Escorial, his severe palace, monastery and library in the foothills of the Sierra de Guadarrama, northwest of Madrid.

Felipe's son, Felipe III, was to hold court in Valladolid for several years, though eventually he returned to Madrid. It was he who ordered the construction of the five-storey Plaza Mayor, later rebuilt three times. Nearby the seventeenth-century Plaza de la Villa, little changed today, reveals that Madrid was at last taking itself seriously as a city.

The death of Carlos II, heirless, in 1700 sparked a war over the Spanish succession, which resulted in the enthronement of the Bourbon Felipe V. When Madrid's *alcázar* burned down in 1734, with the loss of many art treasures, Felipe seized the opportunity to build a lavish new royal palace – today's Palacio Real. The building is still used for government and royal ceremonies, although the royal family lives in the Palacio de la Zarzuela, just to the northwest of Madrid.

Madrid still honours the memory of Carlos III, the most popular Bourbon king, who ruled from 1759–88.

A public spectacle in the Plaza Mayor, around 1700

Madrid in 1854, with the old bullring to the fore

He installed public fountains and laid out the Paseo del Prado, he worked hard to pave and lamplight humbler streets and to eradicate crime.

Spain again became a battleground in the early 1800s, with British forces taking on Napoleon's troops in the Peninsular War, called the War of Independence by Spaniards. Napoleon invaded Spain in March 1808 and invested his brother, Joseph, as King José I. On May 2, 1808, Madrid rose up against the interloper. The war went on murderously but inconclusively for six years. Finally, with the help of the British under the Duke of Wellington, the Spanish expelled the occupying forces. In part, Joseph Bonaparte had meant well, and built so many plazas that *madrileños* nicknamed him *El Rey Plazuelas* – however, the people loathed a government imposed from abroad.

Decline and decadence

The son of Carlos IV, Fernando VII, was seated on his rightful throne in Madrid's Palacio Real in 1814. But the War of Independence and the repercussions of the French Revolution had helped to create in Spain the nucleus of a liberal nationalist party. Power struggles ensued.

The spirit of liberalism prevalent in Europe was tardy in reaching Spain. After many reverses, a democratic constitution was finally proclaimed and constitutional monarchy was instituted in 1874. Alongside this, the Spanish–American War of 1898 marked the final collapse of the Spanish empire of the Golden Age, steadily whittled to insignificance. King Alfonso XIII inaugurated the Madrid Metro and University City, but he was undone by the chronic unrest of his subjects. Neither constitutional government nor dictatorship proved workable, and in 1931 the king went into exile following anti-royalist results in municipal elections.

The Civil War

The 1931 general elections created the Second Republic. Bitter ideological conflicts divided parties and produced factions, and the church became heavily involved.

In 1936, a large section of the army under General Francisco Franco rose against the government. On Franco's side (the Nationalists) were monarchists, conservatives, the Catholic Church and the right-wing Falangists. United against him were repub-licans, liberals, socialists, communists and anarchists. The Civil War developed into one of the great ideologi-cal causes of the twentieth century. Many Europeans saw the Civil War as a crucial

— NOTES —

The Civil War ended with some seven hundred thousand combatants dead; another thirty thousand were executed or assassinated, and an estimated fifteen thousand civilians were killed in air raids. Only now are communal tombs being opened.

conflict between democracy and dictatorship; or from the other side, as a conflict between law and order and the forces of social revolution and chaos. Madrid remained in Republican hands for most of the war, though under siege until March 1939.

Hardship, hunger and cultural isolation dogged the forty-year dictatorship following Generalísimo Franco's victory. Although he kept Spain neutral in World War II, some Spaniards enlisted for Hitler, and Nazi planes bombed civilians in the Basque town of Guernica. Finally, Spain was admitted to the United Nations (UN) in 1955; from the early 1960s, when tourism took off, an economic transformation began that would have profound effects on national identity.

Rubble-strewn street during the Spanish Civil War

When Franco died in 1975, the coronation of Franco's designated successor, Juan Carlos, the grandson of Alfonso XIII, ushered in the so-called 'transition' to parliamentary democracy. The king's commitment to democracy brought Spain into line with the rest of Western Europe, and assured it of future membership in the European Economic Community (now the European Union). In the early 1980s Madrid won a place on the cultural map thanks to its *movida* (see page 8), a street-wise cultural explosion that rejected the stagnation of the Franco era.

Modern Spain

Under Felipe González, Socialist prime minister from 1982 to 1996, Spain stepped onto the world stage. Symbolically, in 1992, Barcelona hosted the Olympic Games, and Seville the World Expo, while Madrid served as European Capital of Culture. González was credited by many as a principal architect of the new Spain, but his party lost power after incessant charges of corruption. In 1996, José María Aznar formed a conservative (Partido Popular) government. During his eight years in power a spectacular property boom began, fuelled by town halls' local control of planning.

On March 11, 2004, three days before national elections, ten bombs tore through three commuter trains at Atocha station in Madrid. Some 201 people were killed and around 1,500 injured. Most of those eventually found guilty were from Morocco, but Aznar's attempt to blame the attack on Basque separatists was one of various factors that created a swing of votes towards the Socialists (PSOE), led by José Luís Zapatero. His reforming spirit in dealing with corruption, ensuring modern civil rights and encouraging a federal state was widely supported, but was dragged down by the government's delayed reaction to the growing economic crisis. By 2011, when elections returned the Partido Popular to power with Mariano Rajoy as prime minister, Spain's unemployment rate was the highest in Europe, and rising. Economic hardships and austerity measures implemented by the government triggered massive social protests, first in Madrid at Puerta del Sol and subsequently in other large cities. The so-called 'Indignants Movement' demanded radical changes in the Spanish politics and turned out to be a springboard for a new anti-establishment left wing party – *Podemos* (meaning 'We can').

In 2014 Spain's King Juan Carlos abdicated and his son Felipe VI ascended the throne, with hopes for a new era for the Spanish monarchy. Nevertheless, it was just the beginning of revolutionary changes. A year later, tired of prolonged economic crisis and the corruption scandals ravaging the main political parties (PP and PSOE), the Spaniards let new formations, including *Podemos* and liberal *Ciudadanos*, enter the parliament for the first time.

Later years of Rajoy's tenure were marked by the controversial Catalonia referendum in October 2017, denounced as illegal by the central government. Violent clashes with police, a deepening constitutional crisis and the region's unilateral declaration of independence eventually led to direct rule being imposed from Madrid. However, the Catalan crisis was not nearly as damaging for the government's popularity as the corruption scandal that saw Rajoy lose a vote of no confidence in June 2018. PSOE returned to power, with economist Pedro Sanchez taking over as prime minister. Sanchez vowed to 'reinstate dialogue' with the Catalan independence movement, but some 45,000 people took to Madrid's streets in 2019 to decry what they saw as Sanchez's conciliatory attitude towards Catalonia, as the country prepared for the trial of separatist leaders; nine ended up in jail. In June 2025, tens of thousands of people protested in Madrid against Sanchez's government, as the ruling party faced a series of corruption allegations.

Chronology

900–400 BC Celtic tribes settle and mix with Indigenous Iberians.

206 BC End of Carthaginian rule in Spain.

AD 711 Islamic armies invade Spain.

852 Muslims found settlement of Magerit.

996 Madrid conquered by Castile.

1109 Muslims unsuccessfully storm Madrid. Madrid wins town status.

1309 Royal Parliament (Cortes) held in Madrid.

1469 Marriage of Fernando and Isabel unites Aragón and Catalonia with Castile to create a unified Spain.

1492 Moors defeated in Granada; Muslims and Jews expelled.

1561 Felipe II establishes capital in Madrid, replacing Toledo.

1606 Madrid renamed capital of Spain.

1701–13 War of Spanish Succession.

1808–14 Peninsular War; Joseph Bonaparte is king.

1874 Restoration of Bourbon monarchy.

1931 Second Republic created after municipal elections.

1936–9 Spanish Civil War ends in Franco dictatorship.

1975 Franco dies, Juan Carlos becomes king.

1986 Spain joins European Community (now the EU).

2004 Ten bombs kill 201 on Madrid commuter trains. Spain's Crown Prince Felipe marries Letizia Ortiz.

Prime Minister Pedro Sanchez

2011 The Indignados occupation of Puerta del Sol attracts world attention. Partido Popular's Mariano Rajoy becomes PM.

2014 Juan Carlos abdicates the throne in favour of his son Felipe.

2017 Controversial Catalonian independence referendum is declared illegal by central government in Madrid.

2018 Mariano Rajoy is replaced by Pedro Sanchez of PSOE.

2019 High-profile trial of Catalonian separatist leaders in Madrid.

2023 Sanchez calls snap elections and forms coalition government despite PSOE finishing second. Spain wins the Women's World Cup.

2024 Spain's national football team wins the Euro and Olympic gold, Carlos Alcaraz wins the French Open and Wimbledon, and Real Madrid win the Champions League and Intercontinental Cup.

2030 Madrid set to host games – potentially including the final – in the 2030 FIFA World Cup.

Busy Gran Vía

Places

Lying at the heart of the sprawling modern city, the parts of Madrid of greatest interest to visitors – both old and new – are remarkably compact. Old Madrid, the city of the Habsburgs, covers a small area that extends east from the Río Manzanares to Puerta del Sol. Almost all of it can be covered in a day or two, including the lengthy visit to the magnificent Royal Palace. The museums that are home to Spain's great art collections, clustered on the Paseo del Prado, are equally worthy of exploration. The so-called 'Golden Triangle of Art', between central Plaza de Cibeles and Atocha railway station, will undoubtedly be the area in which art lovers want to spend most time. Those who enjoy exploring the city's backstreets may like to explore popular old barrios (city quarters) such as Lavapiés, Chueca and Malasaña. Salamanca is more sedate, and Gran Vía is the turn-of-the-twentieth-century avenue that connects central to western Madrid.

Old Madrid

Highlights
- **Plaza Mayor**, see page 34
- **La Morería and La Latina**, see page 36
- **Palacio Real**, see page 39
- **Almudena Cathedral**, see page 41
- **Plaza de Oriente and Opera**, see page 42
- **Puerta del Sol**, see page 44
- **Huertas and Santa Ana**, see page 45
- **Lavapiés**, see page 46
- **Calle de Alcalá to Plaza de Cibeles**, see page 47

Old Madrid, the area spreading outward from the Plaza Mayor, is the city's most historic quarter. After Madrid became the seat of the royal court, this area grew rapidly in the sixteenth and seventeenth centuries. Its streets are full of atmospheric *tascas* (bars) and restaurants, churches, aristocratic palaces and major sights like the Palacio Real (Royal Palace), Plaza Mayor and Puerta del Sol, as well as the Convento de las Decalzas Reales, Madrid's most important convent.

Plaza Mayor

The porticoed **Plaza Mayor ❶**, an architectural symphony of bold but balanced lines, is one of Spain's best-loved squares. Broad arcades surround a cobbled rectangle 200m long and 100m wide (656ft x 328ft). Originally built at the beginning of the seventeenth century, based on the style of Juan de Herrera (Felipe II's architect, responsible for El Escorial; see page 79), the square we know today, with slate roofs, slender towers and facades of brick and stone dates from 1790–1854. The Plaza Mayor may be entered by any of nine archways. Once it was the scene of pageants, markets, theatre festivals, bullfights, religious processions and even trials and executions during the Spanish Inquisition – residents with access to any of the four hundred balconies overlooking the square used to sell tickets for such events. A statue of Felipe III occupies

Plaza Mayor on a beautiful autumn day

San Miguel Market

a place of honour, and the Casa de la Panadería (bakery) is deco-rated with colourful modern frescoes. You can take in the elegant architectural ensemble from a seat at one of the outdoor cafés or during a night-time stroll. A great number of events were held here in 2017 to commemorate the 400th anniversary of the plaza's construction; the square also received a facelift for the occasion.

Leading out of each of the Plaza's arched doorways are narrow, winding streets or staircases. The most famous of these is **Cava San Miguel**, in the southwestern quarter, lined with shops, tav-erns and *mesones* (cave-like bars). If you head for Calle Mayor on the western side, you'll come first to the **Mercado de San Miguel** (www.mercadodesanmiguel.es), a beautiful Art Nouveau food market, polemically revamped as a pricey emporium for buying and sampling food and wine.

Plaza de la Villa

Further along Calle Mayor is Madrid's oldest square, **Plaza de la Villa ❷**, once the seat of the city's government. The fifteenth-century Gothic **Casa y Torre de los Lujanes** (House and Tower of the Lujanes) has an imposing stone portal and Mudéjar tower.

Casa de Cisneros, on the south side of the square, was built in the mid-sixteenth century by a nephew of the inquisitor and warrior, Cardinal Cisneros, and is a fine example of the delicate, ornate style of architecture known as Plateresque. The **Ayuntamiento** (City Hall) dates from the Habsburg era, adorned with towers and slate spires characteristic of the seventeenth-century official buildings common in this district of Madrid.

Iglesia de San Andrés

Beyond Calle Mayor, crossing Calle de Bailén, is **Parque Emir Mohammed I**, where you can see fragments of the old Moorish wall that encircled the Magerit settlement.

La Morería and La Latina

South of Plaza de la Villa and Calle de Segovia is the old Moorish district, **La Morería**, where the intense traffic and bustle of Madrid suddenly subsides. The quiet and pretty square, **Plaza de la Paja** (Straw Square), was the commercial focus of the city in the days before the Plaza Mayor took over. On

┌─ **WHERE TO SHOOT THE BEST PICTURES** ─────────┐

Gran Vía: The city's best-known street (see page 69). Most try to squeeze both the Art Deco Edificio Carrión and the Cine Callao into their photos, with dusk-time best for the surrounding neon display.

Art classics: A photo of *Guernica* (see page 59) at the Reina Sofía is near obligatory; chances are it's going to look a lot like everyone else's photos of *Guernica*, but so what? Alternatively, try Goya's 'Black Paintings' at the Prado (see page 50).

Parque del Retiro: A park full of things to see and snap (see page 61), including a lake and the fairytale Palacio de Cristal.

Hotel Riu: There's a dedicated rooftop selfie bridge atop this hotel, overlooking the Plaza de España (see page 74), with simply jaw-dropping views – you don't have to be staying here to take some photos, but you *may* have to get creative.

Segovia: Heading out of Madrid, this small city is full of great photo ops, with pride of place going to its Roman Aqueduct (see page 90).

Flamenco: You're bound to get some good pictures when watching artists performing flamenco, and some of the more old-school venues are also rather attractive even outside of performance time (see page 104).

└──┘

the south side of the plaza, with its entrance around the other side, is **Iglesia de San Andrés**, splendidly restored (free). Inside is the **Capilla del Obispo**, marking the original burial place of Madrid's patron saint.

Adjoining it is the **Museo de San Isidro**, also known as **Museo de los Orígenes de Madrid ❸** (Plaza de San Andrés; free), built within the restored shell of the palace of the Vargas family, for whom Isidro worked as a labourer. Built around a large patio planted with local sierra trees and flowers, the museum gives a lively overview of Madrid when it was a farming town, using fossils, 3D audiovisuals, artefacts and architectural models.

El Rastro flea market

Just southwest of here is the formidable mid-eighteenth-century **Real Basílica de San Francisco el Grande** ❹ (Basilica of St Francis of Assisi; charge). When Madrid's most important friary was rebuilt in neoclassical style, a dome was added with an inner diameter of more than 31m (100ft), larger than that of the cupola of St Paul's in London. The church's paintings include works by Goya, Ribera and Zurburán.

East of Plaza, San Andrés is a closely packed network of animated alleys and streets: among them, **Cava Baja**, **Cava Alta** ❺, Calle Almendro and Calle del Nuncio. They are home to craft shops and, increasingly, bars or eateries inside old taverns. The barrio was one of Madrid's classic working-class areas and is at its most lively on Sunday mornings when **El Rastro** flea market (see page 100) fills a warren of streets entered from Calle de Toledo, a lively thoroughfare that leads back up to the Plaza Mayor.

On Calle de Toledo stands the **Colegiata de San Isidro** (free). Built by the Jesuits in the early seventeenth century, this church was modelled on that of the Gesu in Rome, and between 1885 and 1993, was Madrid's cathedral. It remains so today in many *madrileños'* hearts. San Isidro keeps many relics, including the revered remains of the city's patron saint, San Isidro Labrador, and a Virgin wearing a military sash awarded by Franco.

Palacio Real

The **Palacio Real** 🄺 (Royal Palace; www.patrimonionacional.es; charge, but free for EU citizens last two hours Mon–Thurs), just west of the Plaza de Oriente, was built in the eighteenth century on the site of the medieval wooden *alcázar* destroyed by fire in 1734. The new grey stone palace, commissioned by Bourbon king Felipe V, was completed in 1755. Set among formal gardens on a bluff overlooking the Manzanares valley, this imperious residence is loaded with art and history.

Guided and self-guided tours of the palace take in only a fraction of the two thousand rooms (more than any other palace in Europe), but many of its highlights. You can also see the formal

The Palacio Real

Changing of the Royal Guard on the first Wednesday of every month at noon (excluding Aug–Sept and during bad weather). The first feature visitors see is the immense **Plaza de la Armería**, which overlooks the valley west of Madrid. The entrance to the palace is via the main staircase – bright, airy and ceremonious beneath an arched ceiling. Each step is a single slab of marble. The Salón de los Halberdiers contains remarkably well-preserved ancient Flemish and Spanish tapestries. The walls of the **Salón del Trono** (Throne Room) are covered by red velvet and mirrors in matching gilt frames. Its ceiling was painted by Tiepolo in 1764. The conversation antechamber, contributed by Carlos III, has four handsome portraits by Goya.

The apartments of Carlos III consist of one lavish room after another. The outstanding **Salón de Gasparini** is named after the artist, Matias Gasparini of Naples, who mobilized stonecutters, sculptors, glassblowers, clockmakers, silversmiths, cabinet-makers and embroiderers to produce this stunning example of the rococo style, in which floor, walls and ceiling swirl with special effects. The **Sala de Porcelana** (Porcelain Room) is an almost-overwhelming display of porcelain, incorporating over a thousand eighteenth-century pieces from the factory that then stood in the Retiro Park.

The regal, extravagant **Comedor de Gala** (Ceremonial Dining Room), built for the wedding of Alfonso XII and his second wife, María Cristina, in 1879, seats 145 guests. Notice the fifteen chandeliers, ten candelabra and eighteenth-century Chinese porcelain jars along walls hung with Brussels tapestries.

Two highlights for many visitors are the early Hapsburg **Botica Real** (Royal Pharmacy) and **Armería Real** (Royal Armoury). Built in 1594, the pharmacy's cupboards line two rooms with matching glass-and-porcelain apothecary jars. The Armería Real (Royal Armoury) displays authentic battle flags, trophies, shields and weapons, a collection regarded as one of the finest of its type in the world. In warm weather leave time for a stroll around the royal

Royal guards on parade

gardens: the formal **Jardines de Sabitini** and wooded **Campo del Moro** (entrance Paseo Virgen del Puerto).

Almudena Cathedral

Adjacent to the palace is the **Catedral de Nuestra Señora de la Almudena** (www.catedraldelaalmudena.es; free), which was finished in 1993 more than 350 years after the cornerstone was laid. The cathedral is constructed on the site of Muslim Magerit, but its most historic surviving feature is the sixteenth-century image of the Virgen de la Almudena, patroness of Madrid, which is kept in the crypt. Guided tours include the climb up to the dome.

On May 22, 2004, the cathedral hosted its first royal wedding, that of Prince Felipe of Asturias and the former journalist Letizia Ortiz.

Inside the cathedral

Plaza de Oriente and Opera

The Royal Palace's front facade overlooks the stately **Plaza de Oriente**, lined with statues of Spanish kings and queens, and the **Teatro Real ⑦**, Madrid's opera house. A guided visit (www.teatro-real.com; charge) takes in the Teatro's opulent salons and the auditorium which was built over a small river, giving excellent acoustics, but construction problems. Behind the opera house in Plaza Isabel II, underground inside the Metro station, you can see the excavated aqueduct, channelling and wash house fed by the river.

A couple of blocks away stands the **Real Monasterio de la Encarnación ⑧** (Convent of the Incarnation) on the small plaza of the same name. Founded in 1611 by Margarita de Austria, this convent's most fascinating feature is the reliquary room, containing saints' bones and other body parts in gilded cabinets. A small phial of San Pantaleón's blood kept there mysteriously liquefies on the afternoon of July 26 every year. In the eighteenth-century church, you may hear the nuns pray or sing, but you'll never see them; they are cloistered behind the grillwork.

Nearby is the **Monasterio de las Descalzas Reales** ❾ (Royal Barefoot Franciscans; www.patrimonionacional.es; charge, free Wed and Thurs pm for EU citizens, by guided tour only). Founded by Princess Juana de Austria, the daughter of Carlos V, in 1566, this palace was transformed into a convent by the architect responsible for El Escorial. The convent, supported by wealthy patrons, accepted only nuns of the highest nobility until the beginning of the eighteenth century. The sisters brought with them spectacular works of art set aside originally as their marriage dowries. Until thirty years ago, the convent was completely cloistered and no visits allowed. Today, Franciscan nuns – a maximum of 33 (the age of Jesus when he died) – remain on the premises, but stay out of sight during visiting hours.

The convent's finest feature is its theatrical granite stairway, splashed with splendid seventeenth-century frescoes from floor to ceiling. On the second floor are rooms with heavy timbered ceilings whose walls are covered with works of art, mostly of religious or royal significance. In one hall hang a dozen splendid seventeenth-century

DRAMA AT THE OPERA

The Teatro Real has had a chequered past. Built on the site of the Plaza de Oriente's washhouse, it opened with a performance of Donizetti's *La Favorita* in 1850, on the birthday of Queen Isabel II, who was an opera fanatic. However, it was closed only 75 years later, when it was found that the stream running beneath it had brought its foundations to the point of collapse. Used as a gunpowder arsenal during the Civil War, the theatre was left closed during Franco's regime – he disliked opera – until it re-opened as a concert hall in 1965. It finally re-opened again, after a decade-long and extravagantly budgeted restoration, in 1999.

tapestries based on original Rubens drawings. The museum also contains outstanding paintings by Titian, Brueghel the Elder and Zurbarán, fleetingly pointed out as you pass through the galleries.

Puerta del Sol

Plaza Puerta del Sol ⑩ is Madrid's busiest plaza and for centuries has been the heart of the city. It also marks the transition between Habsburg Madrid and the city laid out by the Bourbon kings, and after a major renovation project – completed in 2023 – the square has become far more pedestrian-friendly, with the removal of obstacles and steps also making it more accessible. The original gate that once existed here – originally the eastern gate of the Muslim town – was torn down in 1570. Ten streets converge on the plaza. 'Kilometre Zero', a metal plaque set into the pavement below the clock tower, is the point from which distances from Madrid in Spain and Latin America are measured.

The neoclassical brick building below the clock tower, the **Casa de Correos** dating from 1768, houses the regional government. Thousands of *madrileños* gather here for a New Year's Eve ritual. They each swallow a dozen grapes while the clock atop the building strikes midnight, a ritual said to bring good luck for the coming year.

Almost lost in the bustle of the Puerta del Sol is a small statue based on Madrid's coat of arms, which depicts a bear leaning against a *madroño* tree (an arbutus, or strawberry tree). The bear is a symbol of Madrid, and the strawberry tree one of the sierra's most distinctive plants. Whatever time of day you visit this hectic Plaza, you will find it buzzing not only with visitors, but also, often, buskers and locals sharing news and views. In 2011, with the

There are more than two hundred churches in Madrid. In the wider Spanish context they are relatively modern, but include fine examples of Mudéjar and Baroque work.

Puerta del Sol and the Casa de Correos

occupation of the plaza by young Spanish *Indignados*, it became a symbol of the 15M Movement (see page 29).

Huertas and Santa Ana

Southeast of Puerta del Sol lie **Plaza Santa Ana** and Calle de las Huertas, both today lined with restaurants and bars. Once the area had bullfighting associations: bullfighter Manolete was a regular at the *Reina Victoria* hotel, now the *Me* hotel, on Plaza Santa Ana. The square itself is named after the convent that stood here till it disappeared in the 1830s. Also on the square, on the site of an earlier open-air *corral*, is the historic **Teatro Español** (http://teatro espanol.es), while at Plaza Santa Ana 6 is Cervecería Alemana (www.cerveceriaalemana.com), where writers Ernest Hemingway and Lillian Hellman used to hang out.

Bear and strawberry tree, symbol of Madrid, in Puerta del Sol

Reached off the southern side of Plaza Santa Ana, **Calle de las Huertas**, now pedestrianized, has literary quotes set into paving stones in honour of the great authors of the Golden Age and later periods, who lived here close to the theatres where their plays were performed. Not far away, you can visit the **Casa Museo Lope de Vega** ⓫ (Calle Cervantes 11; http://casamuseolopedevega.org; free). The home of Spain's most famous dramatist is beautifully restored as a museum of seventeenth-century life.

Lavapiés

South of Plaza Santa Ana and Antón Martín Metro station is the sloping quarter of **Lavapiés** (literally 'wash feet'), legendarily named after a fountain used for washing feet. In the fifteen century, this was the old Jewish quarter, which has left its mark in winding and twisting streets, the remains of a synagogue under the church of San Lorenzo, and the saintly Catholic street names given when the Jews were expelled. Still one of Madrid's most lively working-class districts, this quarter is now home to a thriving alternative arts scene.

At the heart of the area is lively **Plaza de Lavapiés**. All around the square and in the streets running off it are interesting bars and restaurants. There are excellent Arab cafés and an increasing selection of Indian and Turkish ones – but older locals remain loyal to their traditional Spanish roots and tend to favour dishes such as *cocido*, Madrid's one-pot chickpea stew, *caracoles* (snails), *callos* (tripe) and *oreja* (fried strips of pig's ear).

On the eastern side of Lavapiés spreads **El Rastro**, Madrid's famous Sunday flea market.

Calle de Alcalá to Plaza de Cibeles

East of Puerta del Sol are the city's eighteenth-century quarters engineered by the Bourbon monarchs. **Calle de Alcalá**, once the city's main financial district, leads to the Plaza de Cibeles and the

Facades in Lavapiés

The goddess and her chariot on Plaza de Cibeles

Paseo del Prado. Its spacious boulevards, grand plazas and fountains are interspersed with imposing eighteenth-century blocks that house the head offices or branches of more than a hundred banks, plus insurance companies, and, on nearby Plaza de la Lealtad, the Bolsa de Comercio (Stock Exchange).

On Calle de Alcalá is the **Real Academia de Bellas Artes de San Fernando** ⑫ (www.realacademiabellasartessanfernando. com; charge, free on Wed and national holidays) – the Royal Academy, which is home to a celebrated collection of Goya's paintings, including *Burial of the Sardine*, and a superb self-portrait of the artist in his old age, donated by his son in 1929. Works by Velázquez, Murillo and Rubens are also represented along with a magnificent collection of paintings by Zurbarán, rivalling that of the Prado.

Just before the junction of Calle de Alcalá with the Paseo del Prado sits the **Círculo de Bellas Artes** ⓭, a cultural centre (entrance Calle Marqués de Casa Riera 2; www.circulobellasartes.com; charge), which was built in 1927. The centre's café, replete with chandeliers, vast windows and a grand marble nude by Moisés Huerta (1910), is a favourite among the city's cultural crowd.

The centre's entrance fee includes a visit to the rooftop Azotea for spectacular 365-degree views from the seventh floor.

The point where Calle Alcalá crosses the old city's main north-south artery is a huge, noisy and polluted – yet still impressive – crossroads called **Plaza de Cibeles**. The central fountain shows Cybele, the Greek goddess of fertility and symbol of the city, serenely settled in a chariot pulled by two lions. On the south-eastern side, the **Palacio de Comunicaciones**, inaugurated in 1919 as one of Europe's grandest post offices, has been revamped as the city hall. Located on the southwest corner of Plaza de Cibeles is the **Banco de España** (Bank of Spain) and on the northeast corner is the **Casa de America**, a Latin American cultural centre housed in the plush nineteenth-century **Palacio de Linares** ⓮.

Paseo del Prado

Highlights

- **Museo del Prado**, see page 50
- **Museo Thyssen-Bornemisza**, see page 57
- **Museo Nacional Centro de Arte Reina Sofía**, see page 59
- **Atocha**, see page 60
- **Other museums**, see page 60
- **Parque del Retiro**, see page 61
- **Real Jardín Botánico**, see page 63

The elegant **Paseo del Prado**, the southern kilometre of the great, 5km (3-mile)-long Paseo de la Castellana, is home to one of the world's most impressive cluster of art museums: the Prado, the Thyssen Bornemisza, the Reina Sofía and the smaller CaixaForum. Visitors can stroll down the Paseo's shady boulevard, designed for carriages, head to the Botanical Garden or explore smaller nearby museums.

Museo del Prado

The **Museo Nacional del Prado** ⑮ (www.museodelprado.es; charge, free last two hours) houses one of the world's largest and most prestigious painting collections – and a long-living prestige, since in 2019, the museum celebrated its 200th anniversary. Spanish treasures aside, it includes great works from both the Italian and Flemish schools. The immense collection, ranging from the twelfth to the nineteenth century, was collected and commissioned by Spain's Habsburg and Bourbon kings, private patrons, and convents and monasteries around the country.

The Prado

Despite its greatness, the museum came about somewhat by chance. In the eighteenth century, Carlos III commissioned the architect Juan de Villanueva, draughtsman of the royal palace, to design this neoclassical building as a museum of natural history next to a botanical garden.

After some eventful delays (Napoleon's invasion badly damaged the building), it was decided to use it instead for art. It was inaugurated in 1819 and in 1868 it became El Museo del Prado.

Modernization work in 2007 added a new wing for temporary shows. Pritzker prize-winning Spanish architect Rafael Moneo designed the extension in the former cloisters of the neighbouring Jeronimite church opposite, with splendid contemporary wrought iron doors by Basque artist Cristina Iglesias.

Inside the Prado

The nearby Casón del Buen Retiro, which used to house later nineteenth-century paintings (and later Picasso's *Guernica*, at his own request for it to hang in the Prado), is now the museum's study centre and one of the best libraries.

The Prado owns around 8,600 paintings, but can only display about two thousand of them at any one time (the overflow is either in storage, or on loan to museums around Spain and elsewhere). The result is a stunning collection of master works considered unique primarily for the Habsburgs' collecting tastes, which were unusually broad for the period, cutting across nationalities and cultures.

Visitors often opt for condensed highlights – the illustrated guide sheet facilitates this – and so artworks here are ordered by nationality of schools rather than as a comprehensive tour of the museum.

Highlights of the Prado

SPANISH: The greatest Spanish artist of the Golden Age, **Diego Velázquez y Silva** (1599–1660) was hired by King Felipe IV and became an amazingly perceptive court painter and portraitist. The Prado keeps nearly three-quarters of his paintings. The royal family is featured in his seminal work, ***Las Meninas*** (*The Maids of Honour*). The artist painted himself, palette in hand, at the side of his own masterpiece, in a sense part of the family.

Another vast, unforgettable canvas here is *Surrender of Breda*, commemorating a Spanish victory over Dutch forces in 1625. Chivalry and exhaustion, the array of upraised lances, and the burning landscape communicate a profound pathos, as does his study of Mars, the god of war, hanging close by. Other great works include *Las Hilanderas* (*The Spinners*) and *Los Borrachos* (*The Drunkards*).

'Diego de Acedo' (1644), by Velázquez, in the Prado

Francisco de Goya (1746–1828), another great court painter, had a tumultuous, wildly varied career. His works in the Prado, which trace an extraordinary lifelong evolution of style, form the largest Goya ensemble in the world. Born in Aragon, Goya fled Zaragoza in 1763 for the anonymity of Madrid where he went on to become the king's principal artist.

Goya's 'La Maja Desnuda', radically modern when first revealed

Among the Prado's paintings is **La Maja Desnuda** (*The Naked Maja*), one of Spain's first nudes. Rumours of a scandalous affair between Goya and the Duchess of Alba have long been assumed though art historians now suggest the *maja* – a *madrileño* name for an attractive woman – was Spanish politician Godoy's lover. Goya's most celebrated royal portrait, *The Family of Carlos IV* is daringly honest; only the royal children look remotely attractive. On another level his large canvas, **The Executions of the 3rd of May**, one of history's most powerful protest pictures, depicts the shooting of Spanish patriots by the French in 1808. Goya witnessed this tragedy of the War of Independence from his cottage, and went to the scene to sketch the victims by moonlight. His harrowing 'Black Paintings' – created at home, in old age – are extraordinarily modern in conception and form a focal point in a dramatically lit gallery; many assume that they were a result of a loss sanity (*Saturn Devouring One of His Sons* would seem to be proof of this), but many experts contend that Goya was playing in private with his own lively imagination. Few visitors, even bored teens, leave without trying to make their own minds up about what these pictures mean.

El Greco (1541–1614), born in Crete and long a resident in Italy, became a consummate Spanish painter. He worked in Toledo, his adopted city, for 37 years, toiling at the immense, intensely personal, religious canvases, typically in blacks, yellows and deep mauves, with elongated figures that are his hallmark. *Knight with His Hand on Chest*, an early portrait, is a study of a deep-eyed *caballero* (gentleman) in black. It is signed, in Greek letters, 'Domenikos Theotokopoulos', the artist's real name. The Prado also has several of El Greco's passionately coloured religious paintings, such as *Adoration of the Shepherds.*

Francisco de Zurbarán (1598–1664), a friar and member of the Seville school, combined mysticism and realism. His greatest works are of mythological, religious and historic themes. Monks, priests and saints are portrayed in flowing robes with almost tangible textures. The Prado owns his strained but fascinating battle picture *The Defence of Cádiz Against the English* and his *Still Life*, of a goblet, two vases and a pot emerging from a black background.

Bartolomé Murillo (1617–82), Spain's most popular religious artist of his time, depicted Biblical personalities at ease. His tender and classical religious works brought him international fame, although detractors label his work mawkish.

José Ribera (c.1591–1652) spent much of his life in Italy, where the Valencia-born artist was known as *lo*

NOTES

In the twentieth century, some critics wondered whether El Greco's revolutionary elongated figures were the result of astigmatism.

Bosch's 'The Garden of Earthly Delights'

Spagnoletto (the little Spaniard). His portraits of saints, hermits and martyrs reveal impeccable drawing skills, composition and a keen awareness of the power of light and shadow.

DUTCH, FLEMISH AND GERMAN: Hieronymus Bosch (c.1450–1516), whom the Spanish call *El Bosco*, has three masterpieces in the Prado, including the large, extraordinarily detailed triptych ***The Garden of Earthly Delights***. Daringly mixing erotic fantasies and apocalyptic nightmares, it portrays the terrors and superstitions of the medieval peasant mind. Bosch's wild hallucinations presage similar psychological explorations four hundred years later by Salvador Dalí.

Peter Paul Rubens (1577–1640) pursued a career as a diplomat as well as an artist. Of particular note is his huge ***Adoration of the Magi***, a brilliant religious extravaganza, and ***The Three Graces***, a portrait of fleshy nudes; the woman on the right is said to be Rubens' second wife, Helena.

The finest work of **Rogier van der Weyden** (c.1400–64), the altarpiece *Descent from the Cross*, is on the ground floor. Elsewhere is a famous work by German Renaissance painter **Albrecht Dürer** (1471–1528) – his *Self-Portrait at 26*.

ITALIAN: works by **Titian** (c.1490–1576) include the *Portrait of the Emperor Carlos V*. Depicting Titian's patron in armour, on horseback at the Battle of Mühlberg, it set the standard for court painters for the next century. Titian also produced religious works, but seemed to have no difficulty changing gears to the downright lascivious, as in his *Baccanal*.

Portrait of Emperor Carlos V by Titian

The collection of paintings by **Raphaël** (1483–1520) in the Prado was at one point taken lock, stock and barrel to Paris under the orders of Napoleon, but it was soon returned. Centuries of investigation have failed to uncover the identity of *The Cardinal*, Raphael's explosive character study of a subject with fish-like eyes, aquiline nose and cool, thin lips.

Tintoretto (1518–94) brought Mannerism to Venice. Look for his representations of dramatic biblical stories and, on quite another plane, the close-up of a *Lady Revealing her Bosom*.

Pausing by a painting by Max Ernst, Thyssen-Bornemisza

If you need respite from the vast museum, pop into the neighbouring Jardín Botánico, or head toward Calle Huertas for everyday street life and refreshments.

Museo Thyssen–Bornemisza

On the opposite side of the Paseo del Prado, in the salmoncoloured Palacio de Villahermosa, is the **Museo Thyssen-Bornemisza** ⑯ (Paseo del Prado 8; www.museothyssen.org; charge, free permanent exhibition on Mon and late on Sat). The Thyssen Collection, widely considered to be the greatest private collection after that of England's Queen Elizabeth II, opened in Madrid in 1992. Previously, it hung in Baron Thyssen-Bornemisza's Villa Favorita, at Lugano. His wife Baroness Carmen's impressive personal collection is housed in an extension of the museum.

Admiring Picasso's 'Guernica' in the Centro de Arte Reina Sofía

What makes the collection so interesting is the personal 'eye' behind the eight hundred paintings on display, dating from the thirteenth century to the present day. From the nineteenth and twentieth centuries there are carefully chosen examples of work from key movements: the Paris school, German expressionism, Russian avant-garde and nineteenth-century American painting. Among the classical works are stunning paintings by Fra Angélico, Van Eyck, Dürer, Rembrandt, Hals, Titian, Van Dyck and Rubens. The Impressionists are represented by Manet, Monet, Renoir, Gauguin, Toulouse-Lautrec, Cézanne and Van Gogh.

The representation of artists from the second half of the twentieth century to the present day includes works by Francis Bacon (*Portrait of George Dyer in a Mirror*, 1968), Robert Rauschenberg, David Hockney, Lucian Freud, Roy Lichtenstein and other pop artists.

Museo Nacional Centro de Arte Reina Sofía

Among the cluster of museums on the Paseo del Prado, the **Museo Nacional Centro de Arte Reina Sofía** ⑰ (Calle de Santa Isabel 52; www.museoreinasofia.es; charge, free for 2hr late Mon & Wed–Sat, and Sun afternoon), is the fastest-growing collection. Housed in an eighteenth-century hospital, it currently shows its modern art collection in chronological sections, interweaving work by Spanish and non-Spanish artists and ranging from the turn of the twentieth century up to the present.

The most celebrated work on show is Picasso's monumental *Guernica*, which is displayed behind bulletproof glass. The centre also houses works by Miró, Dalí, Julio González, Juan Gris and Luis Buñuel, and hosts temporary exhibitions. A modern addition, the Edificio Nouvel, has two temporary exhibition spaces, a library, a café and two concert halls.

GUERNICA

Painted in 1937, at the height of the Spanish Civil War, Picasso's *Guernica* was commissioned for the Spanish pavilion of the World's Fair in Paris by Luis Buñuel. In April of that year the Luftwaffe, intervening on behalf of Franco, bombed the town of Guernica (Gernika) in the heart of Spain's Basque region, targeting civilians. Rather than dwelling on the political implications, Picasso directed his intense focus on the suffering caused by violence. Blending techniques from cubism and surrealism, he composed a work of enigmatic yet powerful allusions to earlier Iberian and Spanish art. During and after World War II, the painting came to be seen as a universal expression of anti-war sentiment, and it has also served as a banner for the Basque independence movement. Picasso, who died in 1973, bequeathed the painting to Spain, but stipulated that the legacy should only take effect when democracy was re-established. It was finally brought to Madrid in 1981 after Spain discarded dictatorship.

Atocha

Directly across from the Reina Sofía is the **Estación de Atocha**, a lofty iron-and-glass hangar-like affair modelled on London's St Pancras station, occupied by a tropical garden. In March 2004 Atocha was catapulted into the world news following bomb attacks on suburban trains by Al-Qaeda. In the wake of the bombings Atocha's local station became a shrine of church candles with messages to the bombs' victims. Today the station keeps an underground monument in which visitors gaze skywards, through a giant Perspex cylinder engraved with some of the messages left here in 2004 (free).

The striking CaixaForum building houses a cultural centre

Other museums

Smaller museums in the vicinity of the Prado include **CaixaForum** ⑱ arts centre housed in an old brick power station (Paseo del Prado 36; www.caixaforum. es; charge). Converted by Herzog and de Meuron, this intriguing geometric brick building stands alongside a 24m (78ft)-high vertical wall-garden planted with tropical vegetation. Southeast of Atocha is the **Real Fábrica de Tapices** ⑲ (Royal Tapestry Factory; www.realfabricadetapices. com; charge, guided visits only), which still works with most of the original

Boating on the lake, Parque del Retiro

eighteenth-century machinery. Finally, close to Plaza de Cibeles, the **Museo Nacional de Artes Decorativas** ❷⓪ (National Museum of Decorative Arts; www.cultura.gob.es; charge, free Sun, national holidays and Thurs pm) is a fine collection which includes a spectacular tiled 18th-century Valencian kitchen on the top floor.

Parque del Retiro

East of the museums is the city centre's major green space, **Parque del Buen Retiro** (Retiro Park; free). Until 1868, the park was a royal preserve. Today it is a favourite place for *madrileños* to stroll or relax in the sun. The rowing boats (charge for 45 min sessions) on **El Estanque**, the park's small central lake, are a big attraction all year round. On the eastern side of the lake a semicircular stone colonnade makes a majestic backdrop to a bronze **monument to**

Parque del Retiro's Palacio de Cristal

Alfonso XII, unveiled by his son, Alfonso XIII. The latter survived a bomb attack on the day of his wedding to Queen Victoria's grand-daughter, Victoria Eugenia, grandmother of today's King Juan Carlos, thanks to a message carved on a tree in the Retiro.

Other highlights within the park include the **Palacio de Cristal** ㉑ (Crystal Palace; www.museoreinasofia.es; free), a jewel-like nineteenth-century greenhouse modelled on London's Crystal Palace, that now houses contemporary art exhibitions; the rose garden, **La Rosaleda**, where the old varieties of roses smell as lovely as they look (the best time to visit is April to June; note that at the time of writing it was closed for renovations, and expected to reopen in 2027). In the southwest area of the park, the only public statue in Europe dedicated to the devil, **El Angel Caído** (*The Fallen Angel*), depicts the expulsion of the fallen angel, Lucifer, from the Garden of Eden – a neo-Baroque rendering by the sculptor Ricardo Bellver (1885).

Real Jardín Botánico

A quieter green oasis, next to the Prado, is the **Real Jardín Botánico** ㉒ (Royal Botanical Garden; Plaza de Murillo 2; www.rjb. csic.es; charge). It was founded in 1755, and is laid out around centennial trees, fascinating flowers and rare species. The first dahlias in Europe originated here from seeds brought back from Mexico. In 1803, seven thousand packets of dahlia seeds were sent from here to England, France and Italy for propagation.

At the northwest corner of the Retiro is **Puerta de Alcalá**, a monumental triumphal arch surmounted by warrior-angels, honouring Carlos III. Until the late nineteenth century, this marked the eastern edge of Madrid. Now called the Plaza de la Independencia, the arch or gateway has become a decorative symbol of the city's cultural openness, seen as a monument to its cosmopolitan tolerance.

Recoletos and Castellana

Highlights

- **Around the Paseo de Recoletos**, see page 64
- **Colón**, see page 65
- **Along the Castellana**, see page 65

The **Paseo de Recoletos**, a nineteenth-century prolongation of the Paseo del Prado, runs from Plaza de Cibeles to Plaza Colón, where it becomes the **Paseo de la Castellana**, Madrid's principal north–south avenue, running up to the city's northern limits. Patrician townhouses and palaces give way to ministry buildings from Franco's period, modern apartment blocks and high-rise offices. Several notable museums are housed in this quarter.

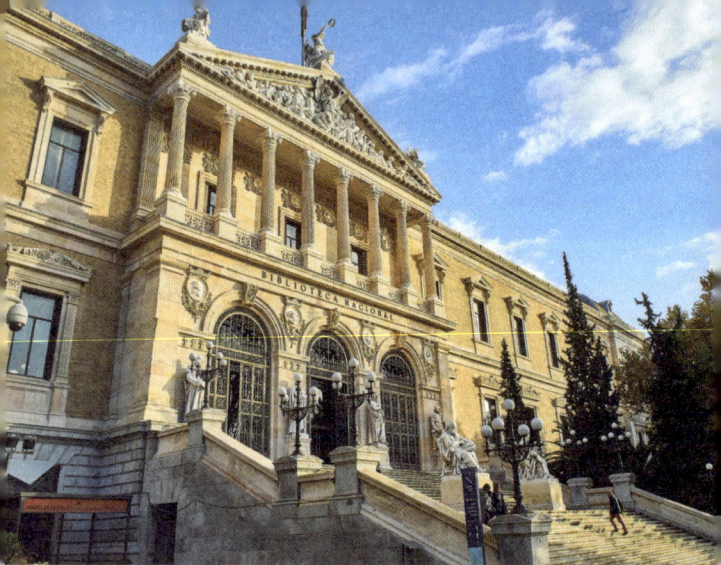

Museo Arqueológico

Around the Paseo de Recoletos

On the eastern side of the Paseo de Recoletos stands the **Museo Arqueológico Nacional** ❷❸ (National Archaeological Museum; Calle de Serrano 13; www.man.es; charge, free Sat afternoon and Sun). The museum's collection of art and artefacts stretches from Spain's ancient cultures – Greek, Roman and Visigothic – to the Romanesque pilgrimage route. One star exhibit is the *Dama de Elche*, a stone sculpture found in Alicante province in 1897 and thought to be 2,500 years old.

Outside the museum's front door is an intriguing underground reproduction of the painted prehistoric scenes discovered in a cave in Altamira in northern Spain.

Recoletos has distinct moods by day and night. Calm during the day, on summer nights its *terrazas* – open-air terrace bars – cater for an elegant well-heeled crowd into the early hours. Among the *terrazas* on the Paseo's west side are the quaint retro kiosks of the traditional **Café Gijón** (No. 21; www.cafegijon.com), an intellectuals' and artists' haunt for over a century; and atmospheric **Café Espejo** (No. 31; www.grancafeelespejo.com).

Colón

Plaza de Colón is a large open space where skateboarders gather to practise among hurried businessmen and pram-pushing mothers. An 1885 statue of Christopher Columbus overlooks a larger modern stone monument to the discovery of the New World. Under the square is the **Centro Cultural de la Villa** (City Cultural Centre) where the Teatro Fernán Gómez hosts seasons of jazz, gospel, flamenco and theatre.

Museo Sorolla paintings

Along the Castellana

About six blocks north and slightly east is the charming **Museo Sorolla** ㉔ (Paseo del General Martínez Campos 37; www.culturaydeporte.gob.es/msorolla; charge). This mansion was the home and studio of Joaquín Sorolla (1863–1923), the Valencian Impressionist painter. It now displays three hundred of his light-filled seaside scenes and landscapes and preserves a small lovingly tended garden.

NOTES

About halfway out along the Castellana is the famous Santiago Bernabéu football stadium, home of Real Madrid. Inaugurated in 1947, it has hosted finals of the Euro (1964) and World Cup (1982), and remains one of the world's top footballing venues. At the time of writing, major renovation works were nearing completion, and the stadium – now sleek, silver and decidedly futuristic in appearance – is set to become one of the most distinctive in the world. Tours are available daily (www.realmadrid.com).

Back on the Castellana, around five minutes' walk further north, are the ornate domes of the **Museo Nacional de Ciencias Naturales** 25 (National Natural Science Museum; entrance off Calle de José Gutiérrez Abascal 2; www. mncn.csic.es; charge). The museum is home to giant skeletons and dinosaur replicas as well as interactive, child-orientated displays on the animal kingdom, anthropological and mineral collections.

Salamanca

Salamanca, Madrid's most sedate city quarter, lies east of the Castellana. It came into existence in the mid-1880s when the city's growing population made it necessary to expand beyond the old city centre. At its heart, presiding over the junction of Calles Príncipe de Vergara and Ortega y Gasset, and in the plaza that bears his name, is a statue of the character responsible for building the quarter, the Marqués de Salamanca (1806–83), José or 'Pepito' to his friends. A financier, politician, lawyer and patron of the arts, his career, a roller-coaster of fortunes made and lost, ended in ruin in 1867.

Before his luck turned for the last time, he developed Salamanca's grid of streets as a residential refuge for the aristocracy away from the city centre. The Marqués also built Madrid's first tramways, which linked Salamanca with the centre of Madrid.

The streets planned by him now have a staid, gentle and sometimes faded air, but retain smart shops and good old-fashioned restaurants.

The Marqués's own magnificent palace, long ago taken over as bank offices, stands at No. 10 on the Paseo de Recoletos. The area is crossed north to south by three major roads: Calle de Velázquez, Príncipe de Vergara and, closest to the Castellana, **Calle de Serrano**, all important shopping streets.

In its understated way, Serrano is to Madrid what Bond Street is to London or rue du Faubourg-St-Honoré to Paris: designer-label land. Here, top Spanish names, such as Loewe, do business alongside foreign arrivals like Louis Vuitton. The streets off or parallel to

Plaza de Toros, Madrid's bullfighting arena

NOTES

On January 23, 1928, a bull being led to the slaughterhouse escaped and ran amok in the Gran Vía, injuring passers-by. Diego Mazquiarán Fortuna, an elderly bullfighter living nearby, tackled the animal and killed it, an act of bravery that brought him contracts in Spain and South America.

Serrano continue the high-end international theme. **Calle de José Ortega y Gasset** is home to Chanel (16), Dior (6) and Hermés (12), among others.

On the eastern edge of Salamanca is the **Plaza de Toros y Museo Taurino** ❷❻ (Bullfighting Ring and Museum; Calle de Alcalá 231; bullfighting ring by guided tour only except on day of bullfights; www.las-ventas.com; museum free). Officially called the Plaza de Toros Monumental de Las Ventas, (and also a venue for rock concerts), this is the place to go to see a bullfight if you can get a ticket (and, it has to be said, if you really want to), or simply to visit the museum of posters, capes, swords, paintings and photos. For those interested in bullfighting culture, there is also a special part dedicated to the famous matador Manolete.

Gran Vía, Malasaña and Chueca

Highlights

- **Gran Vía**, see page 69
- **Malasaña**, see page 70
- **Chueca**, see page 72
- **Plaza de España**, see page 74
- **South of Princesa**, see page 75

The Gran Vía, a concrete canyon of American-style shopping and theatre culture, lies north of Old Madrid. It is bordered on its north side by fashionable Malasaña, Triball and Chueca, which buzz with life by day and night, and on its south side by the Centro's narrow streets.

Gran Vía

The **Gran Vía** (Great Way) was built in three sections, begun in 1910 and completed in the early 1940s, just after the Spanish Civil War. Conceived as a grand east–west avenue, it cut a channel through the crowded, poorer quarters of the city, and was in part designed for crowd control. Until the 1960s, it was Madrid's main commercial centre. Still very active, it has many hotels and high-street fashion stores.

The three stretches of the avenue are well defined. At its eastern end, nearly all the buildings have Art Nouveau details and carved stone decoration. Alfonso XIII inaugurated the construction of this section in 1910, and it was opened in 1924. This section ends at the Red de San Luís, marked by an olive tree planted at the top of Calle de la Montera, recently pedestrianized. Once a sophisticated shopping street, it is now better known for its sex workers, and runs down to the Puerta del Sol.

Gran Vía at night

On the opposite side of the Gran Vía, the **Edificio Telefónica** (Fuencarral 3; free) augurs the start of brash commercialism. The headquarters of Telefónica, Spain's telecommunications

Marble statues of heroes Pedro Velarde and Luís Daoíz on Plaza Dos de Mayo

company, was Madrid's highest building (80m/265ft) when erected in 1929. Its red clock still dominates the night skyline. Inaugurated in 2013, the **Espacio Fundación Telefónica** (http://fundaciontelefonica.com; free) is an art space showing changing shows with an emphasis on new technology. The panoramic views from the elevator are almost worth the visit alone.

From this point, the Gran Vía's second stretch runs to the **Plaza del Callao** – the square is named after the 1866 battle of Callao, Peru. At night, neon lights and videos flash above the cinemas' placards. This is a good spot for buying Spanish books and music at the giant Casa del Libro bookshop (Gran Vía 29; www.casadellibro.com) or at La Central (Postigo de San Martín 8; www.lacentral.com), a playful book emporium with bistro, a children's zone and reading area.

The third section of the avenue, from Plaza del Callao to Plaza de España, of which construction began in 1925, is more modern in character. Hotels, cinemas and hamburger joints predominate.

Malasaña

North of Callao is **Malasaña**, bordered to the east by Calle de Fuencarral and to the west by the Calle de San Bernardo. Malasaña has changed little in its grid-like layout since it was built in the eighteenth century. Still a rabbit warren of narrow streets, it has always had a lively street life. Nothing highlights this better than the 1808 uprising against Napoleon's troops (see page 26). In the last ten years of Franco's rule, it was also the bohemian quarter. These days, by night it still belongs to rock 'n' roll and the city's bar culture. By day it is home to a creative village of small shops offering alternative design, fashion, books, comics, vintage items, fun food and much more.

The heart of Malasaña is **Plaza Dos de Mayo** ㉗ (2 May Square). Both it and the surrounding streets are still populated by pensioners born in the area as well as young people attracted by its traditions. Around here, every street has a story. Calle Espíritu Santo (Holy Spirit Street) once bore a wooden cross in memory of a bolt of lightning that set fire to a whorehouse frequented by the disguised Felipe III. One stormy night years later, Felipe IV walked past the cross with his aides. They were set upon by thieves, and it is said that only the sword of one Don Luís de Haro saved the monarch.

EL DOS DE MAYO

At the heart of Malasaña is the **Plaza Dos de Mayo** (2 May Square), formerly an artillery park connected to the seventeenth-century Palace of Monteleón. On May 2, 1808, during French rule, local people stormed the palace in search of weapons. As French reinforcements arrived, many locals were killed (others were later executed). The most famous victim was Manuela Malasaña, a 17-year-old embroideress who was on her way home when, according to one version of the story, she was stopped and searched by French troops who found a pair of scissors on her. The French, considering these forbidden arms, summarily executed Manuela. The two Spanish heroes of the day were Pedro Velarde and Luís Daoíz, both of whom also died. Their marble statues adorn the centre of the square under the original arched doorway of the palace. May 2 is still an emotive date in Madrid, when the Plaza Dos de Mayo holds an all-day fiesta.

One of the city's most beautiful churches is found in the middle of the quarter: the early seventeenth-century **San Antonio de los Alemanes** ㉘ (www.realhermandaddelrefugio.org; charge) in Corredera de San Pablo. Inside, the walls are covered by stunning frescoes by Giordano, Cuello and De Ricci.

Further south on Calle de Fuencarral (No. 78) stands the **Museo de Historia de Madrid** ㉙ (free), built over the city's snow wells as an orphanage in the early eighteenth century. The splendid Baroque doorway, worth a sighting in its own right, depicts San Fernando, patron saint of orphans. Inside, in the basement, it shows a temporary collection of maps and architectural models of Madrid.

Calle de Fuencarral has become Madrid's main hip fashion zone, with dozens of local and international shoe, clothes and tattoo shops mixed in among traditional art suppliers, pharmacies and ironmongers.

To its west there are scores of bars and clubs in Malasaña. Calle San Vicente Ferrer and Calle de la Palma probably have the greatest number. Colourful nineteenth- and early twentieth-century tiled facades are a feature of the area, and have been incorporated into the fronts of many modern shops and restaurants.

Chueca

East of Calle de Fuencarral, bordered by Calle de Fernando VI, Calle Barquillo and Gran Vía, is the area of **Chueca**. After running the gamut from nineteenth-century affluence to twentieth-century neglect, it has undergone a fashionable renaissance and is now Madrid's elegant reply to London's Soho.

Chueca's characterful narrow streets, with their mass of restaurants, bars, interior design shops, bookshops, arts and environmental businesses, run all the way to Gran Vía. Much of the business life and the buzzing street scene here is LGBTQ+, and the mood is an open one which fills the *terrazas* on **Plaza de**

Chueca ㉚, winter and summer alike, with Madrid's most fashionable people watchers, local and international. Clubs and music bars also abound. Its Gay Pride (Día del Orgullo) in June is one of the summer's biggest events and the quarter's own annual fiesta.

On January 17, animals ranging from pigs to pampered poodles queue with their owners outside the **Iglesia de San Antón** (open for mass only; free), Calle de Hortaleza, to be blessed by the priest. Inside, the church has a fine Goya painting and St Valentine's bones. The church is the only remnant of the old leper hospital, now converted into a modern site of the Architecture Institute, restaurant, swimming pool, library, exhibition space and more.

On the northern side of Chueca is the striking **Palacio de Longoria** ㉛ (Calle Fernando VI 6; guided tours only by appointment, tel: 91-349 9550), Madrid's only flamboyant, Gaudí-style, modernist building, designed as a private mansion by José Grases Riera in 1902, and today owned by the Spanish writers' and artists' copyright association (Sociedad General de Autores). Look up to the top of buildings around here and you will see fine Modernist details: lizards, penguins and other natural details. A few streets away, the **Museo Nacional de Romanticismo** ㉜ (Calle San

Pooches and their owner waiting to be blessed outside Iglesia de San Antón

Mateo 13; www.museoromanticismo.es; charge, free Sat afternoon and Sun) transports you to a bourgeois city mansion in the time of Isabel II.

Plaza de España

As Gran Vía continues downhill towards the **Plaza de España**, two 1950s skyscrapers, **Torre de Madrid** and **Edificio de España**, come into sight. When you reach the centre of the square you find the **Cervantes monument** where many pay homage to the great writer: a stone sculpture honouring him looms behind bronze statues of his immortal characters, Don Quixote and Sancho Panza, astride their horse and donkey, respectively.

Templo de Debod

Calle de la Princesa, which begins at Plaza de España, is actually a northwest extension of the Gran Vía. Tucked away in extensive grounds behind high railings, the neoclassical **Palacio de Liria** at No. 22 is the residence of the Duchess of Alba. The renowned family art collection includes works by Rembrandt, Titian, Rubens, Van Dyck, El Greco and Goya, but it is only open to view on Fridays. Tours are available by prior arrangement only (www.palaciodeliria. com; charge, free Mon mornings with advance booking). Nearby, on Calle Conde Duque, in the old military headquarters is the new modern cultural center with a musical and historical books library, municipal archive and the **Museo de Arte Contemporanea** (http://condeduquemadrid.es; free). Take a look at the **Museo ABC** (http://museo.abc.es; free) on Calle Maniel 29-31, dedicated to the art of drawings and illustration, and located in an old brewery.

South of Princesa

On Calle Ventura Rodríguez at No. 17 is the **Museo Cerralbo** ❸❸ (www.cultura.gob.es; charge, free Thurs pm, Sat from 2pm, Sun) gives insight into the lifestyle enjoyed by the Spanish nobility during the nineteenth century. Don Enrique de Aguilera y Gamboa, Marqués de Cerralbo (1845–1922), was a compulsive collector, traveller and scholar. His town house, built in 1883, was bequeathed to the nation together with thousands of objets d'art. The artistic highlight is El Greco's *The Ecstasy of St Francis of Assisi* (in the chapel). No less impressive are works by Titian, Tintoretto and Alonso Cano in the Galería de Pintura and a fine collection of Spanish *bodegones*, or still lifes. Of all the many grand rooms, the ballroom is undoubtedly the finest.

Beyond the south side of the Plaza de España is **Parque del Oeste**, a green oasis where people come to enjoy the summer and autumn sunsets. It is home to the **Templo de Debod** ❸❹ (closed to visitors for technical reasons until further notice). The ancient Egyptian temple was given to Spain as a gesture of thanks to the Spanish engineers involved in the Aswan Dam project.

Moncloa and the West

Highlights
- **Casa de Campo**, see page 78

At the northern end of Calle de la Princesa is **Moncloa**, home to Madrid's Complutense University. Landmarks here date from Franco's dictatorship: the air force headquarters (inspired by El Escorial) and Madrid's youngest triumphal arch, **Arco de la Victoria**, which commemorates the victory of General Franco's forces, when they took Madrid in 1939 after a two-year siege. Much of the area around it was destroyed during his approach.

Goya's frescoes in the cupola of San Antonio de la Florida

The **Faro de Moncloa** (Avenida Arco de la Victoria, 2; charge) is a 100m (330-ft)-high transmission mast which was built in 1990 complete with an observation deck for panoramic views. Just beyond Moncloa is the **Museo de América** ③⑤ (Avenida de los Reyes Católicos 6, Ciudad Universitaria; www. museodeamerica.mcu.es; charge, free Thurs afternoon and Sun). Its superb collection of art and artefacts from Central and South America includes the Madrid Codex, 56 pages of bark-paper leaves, one of only four surviving examples of the Maya people's writing, and two series of the famous colonial caste paintings. You need at least two hours to enjoy the museum's entire collection which is unique in Europe.

For aficionados of Spanish art, and Goya in particular, a visit to **La Ermita de San Antonio de la Florida** ❸❻ (Glorieta de San Antonio de la Florida 5; http://patrimonionacional.es; free) is a must. Goya's great frescoes, remarkably preserved, covering the cupola and walls of

Teleferico over the Casa de Campo

the eighteenth-century chapel, mark the emergence of his free, impressionistic style after the illness which left him deaf. The narrative piece in the cupola, capturing a street crowd, is regarded as one of his greatest achievements. The artist's tomb was installed in the church in 1919 and in 1929 an identical chapel was built alongside this one so Goya's frescoes and remains could rest undisturbed by worshippers.

Next to the chapel is **Casa Mingo** (www.casamingo.es), one of Madrid's best loved terrace restaurants, and opposite you have access to the walking path along the city's small river, the **Río Manzanares**, which leads back to Principe Pío station and links up with Madrid Río, a vast landscaped riverbank area, with fountains and bridges, running down to the Puente de Segovia. At the far end of it, in Legazpi, is the **Matadero Madrid** (www.

mataderomadrid.org), a modern cultural center located in an old slaughterhouse that hosts art exhibitions and has a theatre and cinema.

Casa de Campo

To the west of the Río Manzanares is another former royal preserve, **Parque Casa de Campo**, forested by Felipe II in 1559. It can be reached by car, bus, suburban railway line, metro (Lago) or cable car (*teleferico*). The **cable car** (www.teleferico.emtmadrid.es; charge) takes you from the top of the Parque del Oeste across the river and into the heart of the park, an enormous heathland of pines, shrubs, gulleys and grassy slopes, where medieval monarchs hunted *jabalí* (wild boar). Among the pines beneath the cable car you can see traces of Civil War trenches from the city's three-year siege, and you may see sex workers touting their wares on the roads that cross the park (this is not a safe area at night).

Visitors can hire a boat on the lake, swim in open-air pools (June–Sept), or visit the **Zoo-Aquarium** (http://zoomadrid.com; charge), where some 150 kinds of animal pace back and forth behind moats, not bars. There's also a funfair called the **Parque de Atracciones** (http://parquedeatracciones.es; charge).

Excursions

Highlights

- **El Escorial**, see page 79
- **Valle de los Caídos**, see page 82
- **Toledo**, see page 83
- **Segovia**, see page 89
- **Aranjuez**, see page 95
- **Chinchón**, see page 96
- **Ávila**, see page 96

El Escorial

One of Madrid's great advantages for visitors is its position as a central leap-off point to explore Castile. El Escorial, the Valle de los Caídos, Toledo, Segovia, Aranjuez, Chinchón and Ávila are all easy day trips from the capital and you can go much further afield in a day by AVE high-speed bullet trains. If you're travelling by car, note that heavy traffic jams are typical if you head out of the city on Friday night and back into Madrid from 5pm on Sunday, particularly in summer and on holiday weekends. A more relaxing option is to use public transport.

El Escorial

A 40-minute drive from the centre of Madrid, or a one-hour train journey, takes you to **El Real Monasterio de San Lorenzo de El Escorial** ③ (www.patrimonionacional.es; charge, free for EU

El Escorial's spectacular gilded library

citizens Wed–Thurs at certain times of year). El Escorial is the material realisation of the obsession of one man, Felipe II. A huge construction, built between 1563 and 1584, it takes its theme from a victory over the French in 1557 at St Quentin (now San Lorenzo's *fiesta* day), and incorporated the royal family's mausoleum. Felipe II, an introverted, deeply religious man, wanted a place in which he could retreat from his duties as king of the world's mightiest empire and be surrounded by monks, rather than courtiers, so El Escorial was designed as an austere royal residence, a library and a monastery for the Order of Hieronymites.

The enormous quadrilateral of granite stuck on to the flanks of the Sierra de Guadarrama is chillingly austere and vast: it has 86 staircases and more than 2,500 windows. Its structure, with interlocking rectangles offset by spiky towers at the corners, was devised in the sixteenth century by Juan Bautista de Toledo and completed by Juan de Herrera.

Despite his reputation for gloomy fanaticism, Felipe II had an eye for art, and some of his best acquisitions have remained at El Escorial: canvases by Titian, Veronese and Tintoretto hang alongside works by Hieronymus Bosch and other masters from Flanders, which was then a Spanish territory. At the entrance to the Habsburg living quarters is El Greco's vast *Martyrdom of St Maurice*. Felipe II's lack of enthusiasm for this painting, now considered a masterpiece, led El Greco to settle in Toledo in search of Church patronage rather than royal commissions.

The suite of royal **living quarters** reflects Felipe's austere personal habits and piety. Everything is sparse in the study from which he ruled an empire and the attached bedroom has views of the basilica's altar.

Valle de los Caídos monument

In contrast, the richly decorated **Royal Pantheon**, located under the altar of the vast basilica, holds the remains of 23 kings and queens of Spain – the latter being admitted only if they had become the mother of a future sovereign. Felipe V, who loathed El Escorial, and Fernando VI are absent, by their own request. The last royal figure to be laid to rest here was Juan de Borbón, who was obliged by General

Franco to cede his rights to the throne in favour of his son, Spain's present King Juan Carlos I. Juan de Borbón died in Pamplona on 1 April 1993 and was interred two days later, earning his place as the son and father of kings, though he was never a king himself.

El Escorial's **library** is said to rank second only to the Vatican's in quality. The gilt edges of the books face outwards on the shelves to preserve the spines. Pope Gregory XII ordered the excommunication of anyone who stole a manuscript from here.

Signs point the way to the **Casita del Príncipe** (Casita de Abajo), set in a park below the palace, and to the **Casita del Infante** (Casita de Arriba), a shorter but more strenuous stroll uphill, following the Paseo de Carlos III (charge for both). These late eighteenth-century pleasure palaces were built for the sons of Carlos III and are furnished as opulently as any of Madrid's fully-fledged royal residences.

Valle de los Caídos

Just around the mountain is another monument of enormous proportions, but far more polemical. After the Spanish Civil War, Franco wanted to build a monument to commemorate those who died during the hostilities. For the site he chose the V-shaped valley called Cuelgamuros known today as the **Valle de los Caídos** (Valley of the Fallen). The most visible part of the monument is a huge cross standing 150m (492ft) high, set upon the summit of a small mountain. Equally grand is the underground **Basilica** open to the public (www.valledeloscaidos.es; free). Carved 240m (786ft) deep into the granite mountain, using prisoner-of-war labour from the Republican forces, the basilica is reached via a tunnel. The tombs of Franco and José Antonio Primo de Rivera, founder of the Falangist Party, occupy a privileged position, making this a place of homage for his followers. Ossuaries in the crypt (closed to the public) contain the remains of tens of thousands of the dead, of both sides, from the Civil War, making private reburial impossible, despite descendants' requests.

Toledo at sunset

Toledo

If you have just one day available for an excursion from Madrid, **Toledo** ㊳, the country's Visigothic capital in the sixth century, is a good choice. Originally a Roman fortress, it reached its zenith in the Muslim period and after the Christian Reconquest by Alfonso VI in the eleventh century, when it became capital of Castile. Alfonso was crowned emperor of Spain and a two-century 'Golden Age' ensued. The court's transfer to Madrid in 1561 triggered the economic decline of the former capital.

To enjoy Toledo's history and beauty at its best you need to work around the massive influx of tourists it receives on day excursions. Even Toledo's renowned steel craftsmen, whose traditional skills such as 'damascening' – cutting pigmented patterns in the metal – are rooted in the city's Moorish heritage, have had to take action

against the producers of thousands of trashy items sold as souve-
nirs. The best way to avoid the crowds and enjoy the historic centre
is to stay overnight.

A good place to start a visit is **Museo de Los Concilios y Cultura
Visigoda** Ⓐ (Iglesia de San Roman; free), which explores the city's
Visigothic legacy. It is housed in the beautiful thirteenth-century
Mudéjar church of **San Roman**, which was probably built on the
ruins of an earlier mosque, which in turn was built on the site of a
Visigoth church. Such are the layers of Toledo's history.

Before the structure of the Church crystallized and Toledo's
cathedral became the symbol of its power, there was a period of
relative tolerance in the late Middle Ages when Islam, Christianity

Toledo's Catedral and Alcázar

Toledo

Estación

Castillo de San Servando

Puente de Alcántara

Rda. de Juanelo

Madrid

Rda. de Juanelo

Puente Nueva de Alcántara

Paseo de Cabestreros

Tajo

C. de Cervantes

C. Miguel

Plaza de la Concepción

Museo de Santa Cruz

Casa de la Cultura

C. Gerardo Lobo

C. Santa Fe

Alcázar

San Juan de la Penitencia

C. General Moscardo

Cuesta de Carlos V

C. Río Llano

Palacio de Benacazon

Plaza San Agustín

Plaza de Zocodover

Plaza San Justo

Hombre de la Magdalena

Plaza Mayor

C. Barco

C. Lucio

C. Núñez

C. Venancio González

BARRIO DE LA ANTEQUERUELA

Plaza del Ayuntamiento

Catedral Primada

Palacio Arzobispal

Puerta del Sol

Mezquita de Cristo de la Luz

San Nicolás

C. la Plata

Hospital del Rey

Hospital de Tavera

Puerta de Bisagra

Santiago

C. Real

C. Alfonso VI

Santo Domingo el Real

Plaza de Santa Clara

San Juan Bautista

San Román

Museo de San Marcos

C. Santo Tomé

Taller del Moro

Santo Domingo el Antiguo

Convento de Santo Domingo de Silos

Plaza de la Cruz

Museo de los Concilios y Cultura Visigoda

Santo Tomé

Museo del Greco

Consejerías

Castillo-La Mancha

Santa Mozárabe

Santa Eulalia

Convento Carmelitas Descalzas

Museo Arte Contemporáneo

Sinagoga Santa María la Blanca

Sinagoga del Tránsito Museo Sefardí

Plaza de la Virgen de Gracia

C. los Reyes Católicos

Puerta de Cambrón

Palacio de la Cava

San Juan de los Reyes

Puente de San Martín

Ermita del Cristo de la Vega

PARQUE DEL CIRCO ROMANO

PARQUE DE LA VEGA BAJA

Glorieta de la Reconquista

Av. Carlos III

Avenida de la Cava

Tajo

0   200 m
0   200 yds

Courtyard of the El Greco Museum

and Judaism coexisted quite comfortably. Their famed *convivencia*, as it is known, produced a cultural flowering expressed in medicine and the sciences, literature and translation, architecture and the arts. In particular, the Mudéjar architecture and decoration created by Muslim craftsmen who stayed in Spain after the Reconquest reached a high point here between the twelfth and sixteenth centuries. It was adopted by the Jewish community, too, after the onset of Christian persecution in the fourteenth century.

   Two historic synagogues stand on the southwestern slope of the city – the **Sinagoga del Tránsito B** (charge), built for Pedro the Cruel's treasurer, Samuel Levi, in the second half of the four-teenth century and today containing the small Museo Sefardi; and the thirteenth-century **Sinagoga de Santa María la Blanca C** (charge). Both show strong Moorish influence in their design, with horseshoe arches, arabesques and glazed tiles. By contrast, all that remains of the Muslim past is the **Mezquita Cristo de la Luz D**, later converted into a church, above the Puerta del Sol; and the **Puerta de la Bisagra**, the main entry point for visitors coming from Madrid.

The **Catedral E** (www.catedralprimada.es; free) is one of Spain's most spectacular sights. It is visible from any part of town thanks to its Gothic tower topped by a spire ringed by spikes. Built between the thirteenth and fifteenth centuries, it is remarkable for its design, the carvings and paintings in its chapels and choir and later accumulated additions. It remains the first seat of the Primate of Spain. The Sacristy contains works by El Greco, Goya, Van Dyke and Bellini. Other highlights include the frescoed chapter house and the sixteenth-century stained glass in the transept.

El Greco's masterpiece, *The Burial of the Count of Orgaz*, is on display in the **Iglesia de Santo Tomé F**, close to the cathedral (www.santotome.org; charge). The artist painted himself into the picture – he's the seventh figure from the left at the bottom, staring straight ahead. Earlier paintings in the **Convento de Santo Domingo de Silos G** where he and his wife were buried – are also of interest. In this area, too, stands the **Museo del Greco H** (Paseo del Transito;

EL GRECO IN TOLEDO

El Greco spent the most productive years of his prolific career in Toledo. Just down the hill from Santo Tomé, the El Greco house – misleadingly named, since the artist almost certainly never lived in it – has been reconstructed and linked to a museum dedicated to his life. Still, it has authentic sixteenth-century furnishings and a tranquil garden that replicate the look and feel of a Toledan house of the era. Several of the master's paintings are on display, among them A *View of Toledo* and *Portrait of St Peter*. The El Greco house was originally built by Samuel Levi, a fourteenth-century Jewish financier and friend of King Pedro the Cruel of Castile.

www.culturaydeporte.gob.es; charge, free late Sat and Sun), refurbished for the 400th anniversary of El Greco's death in 2014, with the recreation of the old painter's house and modern exhibition spaces.

Near the **Plaza de Zocodover**, in the heart of Toledo, is the **Museo de Santa Cruz ❶** (free), a fine Renaissance building displaying more works by El Greco, Ribera and Goya.

Beyond the city walls, in the northern district of Las Covachuela, the **Hospital de Tavera ❶** (free) exhibits works by El Greco, Tintoretto, Titian, Zurbarán and Ribera.

Dominating the city is the enormous **Alcázar ❶** (http://cultura. castillalamancha.es; charge, free on Sun), a fortress destroyed and rebuilt many times since the Roman era. The fortress now houses a five-storey **Army Museum** with displays relating to the dramatic 72-day siege.

Interior of Toledo's Catedral

Travelling to Toledo by train (high-speed services available from Madrid; 35min) will enable you to admire its grand neo-Mudéjar **railway station**, built for Alfonso XIII's visits to the city. In the 1920s, this was the starting point for evenings of the Grand Order of Toledo, a group of surrealists, including Salvador Dalí and Luis Buñuel, who met with the sole object of drinking the night away in good company in Toledo.

If you're driving back to Madrid from Toledo and

Rood screen at Toledo Cathedral

want to make a brief stop, the village of **Illescas** (33km/20 miles from Toledo) keeps five paintings by El Greco, which hang in the church of the local Hospital de la Virgen de la Caridad (Convent of the Virgin of Charity; www.elgrecoillescas.com; charge).

Segovia

Located 88km (55 miles) northwest of Madrid, and easily reached by AVE high-speed train (45 minutes; frequent buses available too), **Segovia** ❸❾ rises majestically from the surrounding plains. The city's setting is picturesque *campo* – wide-open plains interrupted by an occasional monastery or castle – with the slopes of the Sierra de Guadarrama filling half the horizon.

Segovia is a city of great monuments, all testament to epochs of glory: a 2,000-year-old aqueduct, a fine cathedral and a later

Segovia's Roman aqueduct

storybook *alcázar*. It also has dozens of smaller churches, cultural sites and experiences that may be visited seasonally (www.turismo desegovia.com).

The wondrous **Roman Aqueduct** Ⓐ, a work of art and a triumph of engineering, marches right across the entrance of the town. The aqueduct is composed of thousands of granite blocks arranged in graceful arches, sometimes two-tiered, but without mortar or cement. It is nearly 1km (0.5 miles) long, and it rises to a height of 46m (150ft). This is the last lap of a conduit that brought water from a mountain stream down to the walled city. The aqueduct was in constant use for one hundred generations, with only a couple of details changed. In the sixteenth century, a statue of Hercules in a niche over the tallest arch was replaced by a Christian image.

Segovia

C. de los Casasos
Vía Roma
San Justo
Plaza de la Artillería
C. de San Justo

Paseo de Santo Domingo de Guzmán
C. del Cardenal Zúñiga

Convento de Santa Cruz

San Juan de los Caballeros
C. del Taray
Plaza de los Caídos
Plaza San Agustín
Plaza de los Caídos Colmenares.

Acueducto
Romano

A

Plaza del Azoguejo
Madrid

San Sebastián
Museo Provincial·Casa del Hidalgo

Cuesta de S. Bartolomé
Plaza del Seminario
Obispo Gandásegui
Seminario
Plaza del Seminario
C. de Cervantes
Casa de los Picos

Madrid

Paseo del Obispo
C. del Dr. Velasco
San Nicolás
C. de S. Facundo
C. S. Facundo
Plaza de los Huertos
Torreón de Lozoya
C. de Arturo Merino

D

Alameda del Parral
Eresma

Convento de las Oblatas
San Quirce
C. Baja
La Trinidad
Convento de la Trinidad
Plaza San Martín
Plaza de Espejos
Palacio de los Condes de Alpuente
C. de Juan Bravo

San Esteban
Convento de las Dominicas
C. de la Victoria
Palacio Episcopal
San Miguel
C. Serrano
San Martín
C. Cabritería
C. de S. Millán
Plaza Morería
C. de Santo Domingo

Plaza de San Esteban
Ayuntamiento
Plaza Mayor
C. Infanta Isabel

I

Puerta de Santiago

Casa-Museo de Antonio Machado
C. de los Escuderos
Convento de Corpus Cristi

C Catedral

Plaza de la Catedral

Paseo de los Tilos
C. de San Valentín

Paseo Ezequiel González
Madrid

Paseo de San Juan de la Cruz
Paseo de Santo Domingo de Guzmán
C. de la Moneda
Casa de la Moneda

E Monasterio de El Parral

C. de Daoíz
C. Velarde
Paseo de San Juan de la Cruz
San Andrés
Plaza del Socorro
Puerta de San Andrés
C. Leopoldo Moreno

A

Cuesta de los Hoyos

Clamores

Casa del Sol

F Iglesia de la Vera Cruz

Plaza de la Reina Victoria Eugenia

Paseo de D. Juan II

B Alcázar

Cuesta de los Hoyos

N

0   200 m
0   200 yds

The **Alcázar** Ⓑ, Segovia's fairytale royal castle (www.alcazar desegovia.com; charge, free Tue afternoon for EU citizens), was erected on a ridge overlooking the confluence of two rivers, with an unimpeded view of the plateau in all directions. The Romans are thought to have built a watchtower here. The present castle, reportedly the model for the first Disneyland, is a far cry from the simple stone fortress that took shape in the twelfth century. As the fortress grew bigger and more luxurious, it also came to play a significant historical role. By the thirteenth century, parliaments were convened here. The most fanciful and photogenic parts of the castle's superstructure – its feast of turrets and towers – are the work of restoration after a disastrous fire in 1862. A hefty climb up

Segovia's Alcázar

the tower will be rewarded by breathtaking views of Segovia and the valley beyond.

From whatever part of town you view it, the **Catedral** Ⓒ (http://catedralsegovia.es; charge) is a beautiful sight. Its pinnacles, buttresses and cupolas seem to belong to a whole complex of churches. Begun in 1525 (but not consecrated until 1768), this is the last of the great Spanish Gothic cathedrals.

Inside, the cathedral's majestic columns and arches are lit by fine stained-glass windows. Two eighteenth-century organs are spectacularly flamboyant. Less obvious are the altarpieces in the chapels, the most important element of which is a sixteenth-century polychrome *Pietà* by the Valencian Juan de Juan, just to the right of the entrance.

Delicate arches line the cloister, which belonged to a former cathedral that was destroyed and was moved here, stone by stone, in the sixteenth century. The adjacent museum and chapter house contain a number of interesting pieces of religious art and relics, including seventeenth-century tapestries, the Baroque carriage propelled through the streets of Segovia every Corpus Christi (in June), and the reminder of a fourteenth-century tragedy: the tomb of the infant Prince Pedro, son of Enrique II. He slipped from the arms of his nurse as she admired the view from an open window of the Alcázar. Legend has it she scarcely hesitated before she leaped after him to her death in the moat below.

Segovia's main square, the **Plaza Mayor**, combines history with real-life bustle. The seventeenth-century town hall faces the large oblong plaza where shoppers, businessmen and tourists take time out for coffee in the fresh air.

A few streets away to the east, a church much older than the cathedral graces Segovia's loveliest square. La Iglesia de San Martín is a twelfth-century Romanesque beauty with glorious portals and porches (open for mass only). **Plaza de San Martín** Ⓓ, which slopes down to Calle de Juan Bravo, is surrounded

Segovia's skyline

by noble mansions. Next to the church, the building with stark, barred windows was built as a prison in the seventeenth century; it now houses a library. Here and throughout the city, the facades of buildings are subject to elaborate three-dimensional decoration, mainly with geometric forms. The most unusual example, the nearby Casa de los Picos, bristles with pointed protuberances.

Total tranquillity permeates the **Monasterio de El Parral E** (donation), founded in the mid-fifteenth century just beyond the city walls but within easy reach of the centre of town. The architectural details, including a Gothic cloister, are being restored in fits and starts. After a Sunday morning visit, you can hear a sung Mass, with Gregorian chant.

Also just outside the wall and almost in the shadow of the Alcázar, is the stunning **Iglesia de la Vera Cruz F** (free), a twelve-sided structure dating from the early thirteenth century. The knights of the Holy Sepulchre held court in its unique double-decker chapel, surrounded by a circular nave.

Aranjuez

A forty-minute journey south of Madrid by train or bus lies **Aranjuez** ❹, whose setting beside the River Tagus is highlighted by its splendid Royal Palace. The **Real Palacio de Aranjuez** (www.patrimonionacional.es; charge, free for EU citizens Wed–Thurs at certain times of year) was built by Felipe II and rebuilt during the reign of Fernando VI after a fire in 1748 destroyed most of the interior but left the original sixteenth-century structure intact. Carlos IV and his queen, María Luisa, furnished it to the hilt. Here you will see a porcelain-lined room even more elaborate than the one in Madrid's Royal Palace. Goya's portrait of Fernando VII shows him for the brutish dictator he turned out to be. The chandeliers are particularly fine. One of the studies is filled with 203 framed watercolour sketches that make for an illustrated encyclopaedia of life in China during the mid-nineteenth century, with customs, trades, temples, flora and fauna meticulously depicted. These were a gift from the Emperor of China to Isabel II. During her reign, too, the smoking room was decorated in layers of stucco to reproduce the Tower of the Two Sisters at the Alhambra, with the red, green and gold colours that have faded from the original.

But in many respects, the Palace of Aranjuez is outdone by its satellite, the **Casita del Labrador** (Worker's Cottage), a rococo-style pavilion built for Carlos IV in

---

NOTES

On summer weekends you can travel from Madrid to Aranjuez on a special train: the Tren de las Fresas ('Strawberry Train'; www.trendelafresa.es), on which strawberries (*fresas*) are handed out by girls wearing traditional costumes.

┌─ **NOTES** ─────────

The most popular guitar con-
certo ever, Joaquín Rodrigo's
Concierto de Aranjuez was
inspired by the beautiful river
gardens at the Palacio Real. The
music transports the listener
to the palace surrounded by
nature; Rodrigo described it
as 'capturing the fragrance of
magnolias, the singing of birds
and the gushing of fountains'.
└────────────────────

response to the Petit Trianon at Versailles. Situated at the far end of the royal gardens, it is packed with eighteenth-century bric-à-brac.

Aranjuez is also worth visiting for its parks and gardens. The most beautiful are the eighteenth-century Jardín de la Isla and Jardín del Principe (Garden Island and Prince's Garden; free).

Chinchón

The picture-postcard town of **Chinchón ⑪**, 52km (32 miles) south of Madrid and a ten-minute bus or car ride east of Aranjuez, remains surprisingly rural. It is famous for its historic **Plaza Mayor**, used for bullfights since at least 1502 and as the setting for a renowned Passion Play on the evening of Easter Saturday. Surrounded by three-storey wooden galleries, the *plaza* is both rustic and elegant.

Chinchón is famous for its bars, in which you can try the local aniseed-based tipple, *anís*; and restaurants serving charcoal-grilled *chorizo* and meat, which may be cooked with the excellent local garlic, another speciality.

Ávila

From Madrid, road and rail routes climb through spectacular woodlands, streams and rugged peaks to reach Ávila province, a wild tundra-like plateau dotted with wind-eroded shrubs and huge boulders. This austere landscape – a source of inspiration for St Teresa and other saints – is one of the highest inhabited areas in Spain: the city lies at 1,130m above sea level, and parts of the surrounding area are more elevated still.

Its provincial capital, located approximately 100km (60 miles) northwest of Madrid, is the medieval walled city of **Ávila** ㊷ (www.avilaturismo.com). Ávila is the highest provincial capital in Spain so until as late as April it can be bitterly cold up there. The **Muralla**, or city wall – over 2km (1.2 miles) long and with no less than 88 watchtowers and nine gates – is the best preserved in Europe. It may be climbed via two points of access, El Alcázar and Casa

The medieval walls of Ávila

de Las Carnicerías (http://muralladeavila.com; charge), now the tourist office. The apse of the **Catedral** (http://catedralavila.es; charge) sticks out to form a part of these fortifications. The city has been a magnet for pilgrims ever since the late sixteenth century, as the birthplace of St Teresa, the great reformer of the Carmelite Order. Visitors can see Teresa's birthplace, now marked by a seventeenth-century church; the convent where she lived much of her life, the Monasterio de Encarnación; and the Convento de San José, the first she founded in the city.

Other notable sights include the **Basílica de San Vicente**, built on the site where San Vicente and his two sisters were martyred in the fourth century; and the fifteenth-century Monasterio de Santo Tomé, with its three haunting cloisters and marble tomb of Fernando and Isabel's only son, Don Juan, who died aged 19.

Flamenco performance

Things to do

Shopping

As the capital city of a major European country, it's no surprise that many visitors to Madrid end up taking far more from the place than they brought in. While many of the major Spanish clothing brands are (don't say this too loudly) actually headquartered in Barcelona, they're all present and correct here too – as is department-store behemoth El Corte Inglés, which has branches all over the city, as well as its own headquarters.

Where to shop

Madrid's major department stores are located in the centre between the Puerta del Sol and Callao, and along the Gran Vía. More select designers line Calle de Serrano and its adjoining streets in Salamanca. Calle del Prado, La Latina and Puerta de Toledo are good for antiques. For high-street shops try Calle del Arenal, Sol, Calle de Preciados, Gran Vía and Calle de la Princesa. Calle Fuencarral is the city's main drag for hip young fashion from home and abroad, with more expensive one-off designs in Chueca in newer alternative shops scattered through Malasaña and its subzone Triball.

Among Madrid's central shopping centres, **La Vaguada** (Avenida Monforte de Lemos s/n, Barrio del Pilar; www.enlavaguada.com), in northern Madrid, is a multi-level complex with three hundred shops, bars, restaurants and cinemas. **ABC Serrano** (Calle de Serrano 61; http://abcserrano.com) is a fair bit smaller but the most central major mall, with selected stylish shops, cafés and restaurants.

Only shopping centres and department stores are guaranteed to stay open through the day. Opening hours are generally Monday–Friday, 9 or 10am until 1.30pm or 2pm, and 4pm or 5pm until 8pm. On Saturday, stores tend to open from 9.30am until 1.30pm. Sunday opening has taken off in the city centre, particularly around Puerta del Sol and Gran Via, but is not yet general through the city.

┌─ THE RASTRO ───────────────

On Sunday morning Madrid's most famous street market, El Rastro, selling everything from antiques, books and fashion to pets and coal-burning stoves, spreads through Lavapiés from Tirso de Molina to Ronda de Embajadores. A good starting point for exploring the quarter is the Plaza del Cascorro, while further down the Ribera de Curtidores – the market's main avenue – is the *rastro* itself, the slaughterhouse after which the market is named.

Some of the most interesting finds are on and around the Plaza General Vara del Rey, where antiques stalls and shops sell second-hand cameras, books and postcards. If you seriously want to buy, arrive by 9.30am. By midday the streets are packed. Be on the alert for pickpockets – this is unfortunately a notorious place for thieving.

Leave time for some tapas in one of the busy bars. El Rastro starts to pack up at about 3pm.

What to buy

There's no shortage of items to take home, from traditional Spanish fans to foodstuffs or cutting-edge fashions.

Books: There's an outdoor second-hand book stand open daily on Pasadizo de San Ginés, off Calle del Arenal, and on Cuesta de Moyano, near Atocha, at weekends. From late May, a book fair takes over the Retiro for several weeks. Antonio Machado (Marqués de Casa Riera 2 and Plaza de las Salesas; www.machadolibros.com) is a good Spanish bookshop. La Central de Callao (Postigo de San Martín; www.lacentral.com) stocks gifts, cards and magazines as well as a huge array of carefully selected books.

Crafts: Casa Hernanz (Calle Toledo 18; www.casahernanz.es) specializes in espadrilles (*alpargatas*), and Antigua Casa Talavera (Calle de Isabel la Católica 2; www.antiguacasatalavera.com) in ceramics. Casa Yustas (Pl Mayor 30; www.casayustas.com) is the oldest hat shop in Madrid, having made them here since 1894, while Guitarras Ramírez (Calle de la Paz 8; www.guitarrasramirez.

com) can go a few years better, having made hand-crafter flamenco guitars since 1882.

Antiques: Head to the Rastro. In the nearby streets are more solid establishments dealing in old objets d'art.

Fashion: Spanish fashion has produced major brands and designers for the last couple of generations. Look for Hoss Intropia (Calle de Goya 29; www.hossintropia.com), Loewe (Calle de Serrano 34; loewe.com) and Camper (Calle de Serrano 24; camper.com). For high-street and budget fashion, explore Calle Fuencarral. Zara's largest branch is at Gran Vía 34 (www.zara.com), and quite a significant chunk of international visitors end up buying a humorous t-shirt at Citees (Gran Vía 60, among other branches; www.citees.es).

Flamenco: Music, clothes and instruments are found at El Flamenco Vive (Calle del Duque de Fernán Núñez 5; www.elflamencovive.com), close to the Prado.

Food and drink: The best place to buy a bottle of wine is Bodegas Mariano Madrueño (Calle del Postigo de San Martín 6; www.marianomadrueno.es), which was established in 1895; also think about investing in some Pacharán (aniseed liqueur with sloe berries). The municipal markets are an unmissable experience for food lovers (Anton Martín in Lavapiés and La Paz in Salamanca are

Fans for keeping cool

Outdoor bookshop on Pasadizo de San Gines

good examples). The gourmet food departments of El Corte Inglés have a good range too.

   Leather: Salvador Bachiller (Gran Vía 65 and other branches; www.salvadorbachiller.com) makes stunning bags, suitcases, wallets and other items in a huge range of colours.

Nightlife

Madrid nightlife is hectic, fast-moving and carries on all night. In the early 1980s, *la movida*, the arts and nightlife nurtured by the socialist mayor, Enrique Tierno Galván, created such a sense of street fiesta that exhausted people would sigh, *Madrid me mata* (Madrid is killing me). Constantly in search of the ultimate in *marcha*, or fun, young *madrileños* flock into the city centre after work, usually from Thursday to Saturday and at least until sunrise.

Good starting points for an evening stroll are the *cervecerías* on the Plaza Santa Ana (sedate), the central boulevard of the Paseo del Prado (smart), or the *tascas* and *tavernas* in Huertas (young), where you can have a bite to eat before things get going in the clubs and bars. In Malasaña, Plaza Dos de Mayo is peppered with alternative bars; while Chueca, to the north of Gran Vía, the vibrant centre of Madrid's LGBTQ+ scene, is the hip equivalent of New York's Soho, with dozens of gay and hetero bars, clubs and restaurants.

Madrid nightlife provides a wealth of cultural experiences. Our top choices are listed below:

Live music: There are plenty of places in Madrid for live jazz and Latin music. **Café Central** (Plaza del Ángel 10; www. cafecentralmadrid.com) is a long-standing jazz café near Plaza de Santa Ana, with nightly music. **Blackbird** (Calle de las Huertas 22; www.blackbirdrockbar. com) has a more wide-ranging line-up including jazz, reggae and blues. **Clamores** (Albuquerque 14; www.salaclamores.es) also has interestingly eclectic programming.

Madrileños enjoying a concert

After-hours clubs: Venues, and their styles, change all the time. Here's a sample of some highlights: **Monnalisa Madrid** (Calle de Núñez de Arce 8), for hip-hop and rock; **Changó** (Covarrubias 42;

FLAMENCO

Spain's most unique art form is flamenco, built around its song, guitars, and – perhaps best known – its dance with percussive heels. Pure flamenco, which has grown around *cante jondo* (deep song) deals with human dramas of t, love and death in a slow, piercing manner. You can watch flamenco in clubs across the capital, including: **Tablao de la Villa** (Calle Torija 7; www. tablaodelavilla.com; Metro: Santo Domingo); **Corral de la Morería** (Calle de la Morería 17; www.corraldelamoreria.com; Metro: Opera) and **Las Tablas** (Plaza de España 9; www.lastablasmadrid. com) which offers a more modern setting than traditional flamenco shows. However, many of the best performances are given in theatres and concert halls – check the newspaper for dates.

www.changomadrid.com), for concerts and club nights; **Teatro Kapital** (Calle Atocha 125; www.teatrokapital.com), for seven floors of clubbing till dawn; **Sala El Sol** (Calle Jardines 3; www. salaelsol.com), a legendary *movida* venue great for indie, rock and alternative music.

Culture

Classical music, opera and dance: As home to the National Orchestra, the Spanish Radio and Television Symphony, the Compañía Nacional de Danza (contemporary), the Ballet Nacional de España, and the city's and region's orchestras and dance companies, Madrid has an exceptional calendar of concerts, recitals and dance events.

Madrid's opera house, the **Teatro Real**, features big-name productions (Plaza Isabel II; www.teatroreal.es).

The **Auditorio Nacional de Música** (Príncipe de Vergara 146; www.auditorionacional.mcu.es) has excellent seasons of recitals and concerts, including experimental contemporary music and flamenco, throughout the year.

The **Teatro de la Zarzuela** (Calle de Jovellanos 4; http://teatrodelazarzuela.mcu.es) and **Teatros del Canal** (Calle Cea Bermúdez 1; www.teatroscanal.com) are Madrid's main contemporary, classical and world dance venues.

Theatre: Spain's dramatic tradition is long and glorious. In dozens of Madrid theatres, classical and contemporary foreign and Spanish works are performed. Among those with the greatest critical acclaim are the following: **Teatro de Abádia** (Calle Fernández de los Ríos 42; www.teatroabadia.com), at the former Church of La Sagrada Familia, offers quality contemporary drama. **Teatro de la Comedia** (Calle del Príncipe 14; www.teatroclasico.mcu.es) puts on classic Spanish works, by playwrights such as Federico García

Performance at the Teatro de la Zarzuela

Lorca and Lope de Vega. **Teatro Español** (Calle del Príncipe 25; www.teatroespanol.es) and its former slaughterhouse space, the **Matadero** (Plaza de Legazpi 8; www.matadermadrid.org), set the pace for excellent classic and contemporary international and home-grown theatre.

Cinema: Details of subtitled films shown in their original language (*version original* or VO) are best perused on the websites of daily papers such as *El País* (www.elpais.es) and in *El Mundo's* Friday magazine *Metropoli* (www.elmundo.es/metropoli.html). The main cluster of VO cinemas, totalling eighteen screens in all, is on Martín de los Heros and Princesa (Cines Yelmo, Princesa, Renoir Plaza de España and Renar Princesa).

Champion's League match between Atlético Madrid and Real Madrid

Teletickets: Most theatre, dance, opera and some cinema tickets can be bought online. As well as the international regulars, try www.entradas.com or www.elcorteingles.es/entradas.

Outdoor activities

Basketball: Games are held in the Real Madrid Baloncesto installations, north of the Plaza de Castilla, or in the Palacio de Deportes on Avenida Felipe II. Real Madrid are almost as dominant in the basketball league as they are in La Liga.

Fútbol (football/soccer): The world's number one sport is a passion in

Spain. The two big Madrid teams are **Real Madrid** and **Atlético Madrid**. Real Madrid play their matches at the recently renovated Estadio Santiago Bernabéu, Av de Concha Espina (Metro: Santiago Bernabéu; www.realmadrid.com). Atlético Madrid play at the Wanda Metropolitano, Av de Luis Aragonés (www.atleticodemadrid.com), on the way to Barajas airport.

Golf: There are 22 golf courses in the Madrid area. Greens are open to non-members on payment of a substantial greens fee. The best source of information is the Real Federación Española de Golf (www.rfegolf.es).

Skiing: From December to April, the Guadarrama mountains north of Madrid become a ski area. The scenery and facilities are first-rate, and all equipment may be hired. The most highly developed resort, with five ski-chairs and six ski-lifts, is Navacerrada (www.puertonavacerrada.com), only 52km (32 miles) from Madrid. Expect the slopes to be packed when there is snow. **Valdesquí**, N601, 150km (92 miles) from Madrid, has six ski-lifts, a ski-school and a ski-tow (www.valdesqui.es). For more details, see www.infonieve.es.

Elsewhere in Madrid, various sports facilities cater to many interests. You'll find tennis courts, polo grounds, squash courts, swimming pools and riding stables.

Madrid for children

The **Casa de Campo**, with its teleférico (cable car), funfair (Parque de Atracciones, see page 78), lake and open-air swimming is a good option on hot days. Also within the Casa de Campo, there's the **Madrid ZooAquarium** (www.zoomadrid.com). The year-round circus at **Circo Price** (Rda de Toledo 35; www.teatrocircoprice.es) is a reliable choice too.

Attractions in the **Parque del Buen Retiro** include marionette shows at noon on Sundays and rowing on the lake (see page 61).

At **Safari Madrid** (Aldea del Fresno, National Highway V, near Navalcarnero; www.safarimadrid.com), elephants, rhinos, lions and

Festival of San Isidro

zebra roam freely, and you can also get close up to birds of prey, insects and reptiles.

Closer to the city is **Faunia** (Avenida de la Comunidades 28, Metro: Valdebernardo; www.faunia. es), a hugely successful theme park simulating a variety of ecosystems and their fauna.

Aquopolis (Avenida de la Dehesa, Villanueva de la Cañada; mid-June–Sept; https://villanueva. aquopolis.es) is a large waterpark with wave pools, shoots, cascades and toddlers' pools. Free buses go from the city centre; check the website for details.

Another attraction is the **Planetario de Madrid** (Planetarium; Parque Tierno Galván; www.planetmad.es; Metro: Méndez Álvaro), where shows start at 5.30pm and 6.30pm Tue–Fri and 11am, noon, 1pm, 5.30pm and 6.30pm at weekends and holidays. The **National Museum of Natural Sciences** (Calle José Gutierrez Abascal 2; www.mncn.csic.es), with thousands of minerals, algae, plants, animals of all kinds, stones, tools and arms from various cultures and ages, will keep children busy for hours.

Located halfway between Madrid and Aranjuez, at San Martín de la Vega, **Parque Warner Madrid** (Ctra M301 km 15.5, www. parquewarner.com) offers five themed areas incorporating sets and characters from Warner Brothers films and cartoons. Among the attractions is an 80kmh (50mph) roller-coaster.

Calendar of events

As you plan your excursions, it is worth checking additional details of festivals and fairs with tourist information offices.

January 6 *Día de los Reyes* (Three Kings Cavalcade). Procession commemorating the kings' pilgrimage to meet baby Jesus.

January 17 *San Anton*. Blessing of pets and animals at San Anton church, Calle Haraleza.

February *Carnaval* (week before Lent). Celebrated with the *Entierro de la Sardina* (Burial of the Sardine) on Paseo de la Florida.

February ARCOmadrid (Contemporary Art Fair; late Feb), Spain's largest international art fair.

March/April *Semana Santa* (Holy Week). Every town and city has striking processions and unforgettable spectacles.

May *Fiestas de San Isidro* (St Isidore the Husbandman). Half a month of neighbourhood parties, plays, concerts and daily bullfights.

June *Corpus Christi* (sixty days after Easter). The Spanish primate leads a solemn religious procession through the medieval streets.

June *Camuñas* (Toledo Province; mid-June). An ancient religious play is presented in mime, with spectacular costumes.

June 23 *Fiestas de San Juan* and *San Pedro*. Dances, bullfights, fireworks.

July *Ávila* (early July). Outdoor festival with poetry, art, theatre, sports and bullfights.

July–August *Veranos de la Villa*. Open-air festival of music and dance in central Madrid venues.

August *Castizo* fiestas, the traditional fiestas of San Caeyetano, San Lorenzo and La Virgen de la Paloma, with much of the activity taking place around the Plaza de la Paja and the Jardines de las Vistillas.

August 15 A major national holiday with many local celebrations.

October–November *Festival de Otoño*. The city's biggest cultural festival includes international theatre, jazz, dance and other events.

December 31 *Nochevieja*. Celebration in Puerta del Sol; grapes are swallowed between each chime of the clock.

Food and drink

Madrid is a food lover's city: its restaurants are for those with every kind of budget, and you can sample regional specialities from around the country, plus world cuisine from Latin America to Asia; in keeping with many foodie cities worldwide, the recent emphasis has been on higher-end offerings, with Michelin stars playing an even more pivotal role than usual in shaping the scene. On the other side of the gastronomic spectrum, you cannot miss the city's take on the *tapeo*, the tapas crawl. Regional cuisine varies greatly, but Spanish cooking is never overly spicy; however, it is garlicky and liberally salted.

Cocido madrileño consists of a broth and platter of meat and veg

Top 10 things to try

Here's a small rundown of the best things to try when you're in Madrid, starting with Castilian specialities, then other Spanish fare, and finishing with drink suggestions.

1. Cocido madrileño

Cocido madrileño is one of many regional variations of the originally medieval, possibly Jewish, one-pot stew found all over Spain. The meal often starts with *sopa de cocido*, the broth resulting from boiling the ingredients for the next course, before moving to the *cocido* itself: beef, cured ham, sausage, chickpeas, cabbage, onion and potatoes.

2. Sopa de ajo

Another local speciality is a Castilian soup known as *sopa de ajo*, or garlic soup. At the last moment, a raw egg is added to the soup, and by the time it reaches the table, the egg is well poached.

3. Callos a la madrileña

Callos a la madrileña is stewed tripe – try it if you like spicy-hot tomato sauce (and, of course, tripe). For a lighter speciality, try *besugo al horno*, baked sea bream, once a Christmas dish.

4. Bocatas de calamares

So popular are these calamari sandwiches with *madrileños* that you may forget that their city is nowhere near the sea.

5. Patatas bravas

Not so long ago, one airline was advertising its flights from mainland Spain to the Canary Islands as being 'from the land of *patatas bravas* to the land of *papas con mojo*', which shows just how integral they are to local food culture – they're cheap as chips, and indeed something like a cubed version of chips, smothered with a spicy sauce. (Try to find somewhere serving Canarian *mojo* sauce at some point, though – a potential future hipster trend.)

6. Paella

From Valencia comes one of Spain's great dishes. Paella is named after the flat metal pan in which rice is cooked with either meat or fish – traditionally not both together – plus garlic, saffron and peppers. Spaniards think of paella, and other rice dishes (*arroces*), as lunchtime dishes.

7. Basque food

A wide variety of sophisticated fish dishes come from the Basque country. Try *bacalao al pil pil* (salt cod in hot garlic sauce), *merluza a la vasca* (hake in a casserole with a thick sauce) or an extravagant luxury, *angulas a la bilbaína* (eels in a spicy olive oil and garlic sauce). However, it's also easy to track down places serving the most famed Basque eats – *pintxos*, a range of snacks mostly spiked onto slices of bread with a toothpick.

8. Churros

These snacks are now popular worldwide, but they're almost always better in Spain, and there's a pleasing local angle in this particular city – it is a *madrileño* custom to finish a late night with *chocolate con churros* (hot chocolate with deep-fried loops of batter). However, they're also a popular breakfast – you can dunk churros in your coffee, or eat them as Spaniards do, with extremely thick, strong hot chocolate.

CHOCOLATE CON CHURROS

Chocolatería San Ginés, Pasadizo San Ginés 7; https://chocolateria sangines.com.
Muñiz, Calle de Calatrava 3.

Chocolate con churros

9. Wine

Wine menus today generally offer bottles from many Spanish denominations of origin: La Rioja, Navarra, Ribera del Duero, Jumilla, Somontano and Madrid are among the most popular. Also try cava, sparkling wine from Catalonia – Spain's answer to champagne. If you just say *tinto* (red) or *blanco* (white) when asked for your choice of *vino*, you'll be given the house wine, which may come in a glass, bottle or be decanted into a jug.

10. Vermouth and sherry

Though vermouth is most readily associated with Italy and France, it's arguably now an even bigger deal in Spain; as elsewhere, *vermut* is typically consumed as an aperitif, and you'll find an array of simple, atmospheric places specializing in the stuff around Puerta del Sol. Sherry (*Jerez*), from Jerez de la Frontera in Andalucia, is delicious when well kept. Pale, dry *fino* is drunk chilled as an apéritif and also with soup and fish courses, while the rich, dark *oloroso* or PX is a good digestif.

Essential information

Mealtimes

Madrileños eat lunch and dinner late by most standards. Lunch usually isn't begun until 2 or 3pm and friends often meet for dinner at 9.30–10pm. Outside local hours, you are likely to find yourself dining alone. Swing into local habits and pace yourself, Spanish style, by grazing on tapas at your normal dinner time.

San Miguel market at night

Restaurants and menus

Spaniards traditionally eat three courses at both lunch and dinner. However, it's not uncommon to share a first course, or to order *un sólo plato* (just a main course), if you're not that hungry. Many restaurants offer bargain lunchtime set menus called the *menú del día*. For a fixed price, you'll get a choice of first course, a main dish and dessert or coffee, plus a glass of either wine (or more), beer or bottled water, and bread.

TAPAS AND EL TAPEO

Tapas – the small snacks for which Spanish bars and cafés are renowned – are one of Spain's great contributions to world cuisine.

The list of tapas available is almost endless, but some of the more common options include *aceitunas* (olives), *chorizo* (cured sausage), *champiñones* (mushrooms, usually fried in garlic), *queso* (cheese), *albóndigas* (meatballs), *croquetas* (croquettes of fish or chicken), *morcilla* (blood sausage), and the classic *tortilla española*, an omelette with potatoes fried in olive oil until golden.

A small plate is called a *tapa*; a larger serving, meant to be shared, is a *ración;* and half of this, a *media-ración*. To substitute for a conventional main course, choose perhaps three different items. Bars specializing in tapas are places where tapas grazing (*el tapeo*) is the order of the day. Two good central areas are La Latina and Huertas, but there are good bars everywhere. Bear in mind that these days *tapas* are rarely free, and do not come cheap.

More than two centuries old, with bulls' heads and other taurine memorabilia on the walls, **Taberna de Antonio Sánchez** (Mesón de Paredes 13; www.tabernaantoniosanchez.com) is legendary. **Taberna Almendro 13** (Calle Almendro 13; www.taberna almendro13.com) is a great corner bar specializing in *fino* and *manzanilla* (dry sherry) and serving a wide variety of tapas and *raciones* to a noisy local crowd. **Casa Labra** (Calle de Tetuán 12; www.casalabra.es) is a great old spot near the Puerta del Sol, where the Socialist party was founded, and still serves homemade salt-cod *croquetas* and *soldados de Pavia* (salt cod fried in batter).

Restaurants feature a grading system, from five forks to one, marked on the door of the restaurant. The system is an indication of price, and grades the facilities and service, not the quality of the food.

While restaurants offer a full menu, often with a fixed-price menu available, *cafeterías* usually focus on *platos combinados*, which combine main courses and accompaniments such as steak, eggs, chips and salad served on the same plate.

Cocktail hour

Most bars and *cervecerías* (draft beer bars) also serve tapas, sandwiches (*bocadillos*) or limited *platos combinados*. In summer their pavement terraces will look alluring, but remember, prices are higher if you sit at a table or outside rather than at the bar.

The most insignificant meal of the day in Spain is generally breakfast, except at hotels, which offer continental breakfasts or buffets.

Opening hours and payment

Many restaurants close for at least one day a week, often Sunday evening and all day Monday. Old-fashioned businesses close for some of August, and many bars close between lunch and dinner.

For payment, almost all places now accept credit cards, and an increasing number won't take cash. Remember that for tapas, as well as meals, you generally pay at the end.

To help you order…

Could we have a table ¿**Nos puede dar una mesa, por favor?**
Do you have a set menu? ¿**Hay un menú del día?**
The menu, please **La carta, por favor**
The bill, please **La cuenta, por favor**
I'd like a/an/some… **Me gustaría pedir…**

The basics…

beer **cerveza/caña**
bread **pan**
cutlery **los cubiertos**
dessert **postre**
fish **pescado**
fruit **fruta**
glass **vaso/copà**
ice cream **helado**
meat **carne**
mineral water **agua mineral**

napkin **servilleta**
plate **plato**
potatoes **patatas**
rice **arroz**
salad **ensalada**
sandwich **bocadillo**
sugar **azúcar**
tea **té**
water (chilled) **agua (fresca)**
wine **vino**

…and read the menu

albondigas meatballs
almejas clams
anchoas anchovies
atún/bonito tuna
bacalao cod
calamares squid
cangrejo crab
caracoles snails
cerdo pork
chuleta chop/cutlet
cordero lamb
entremeses hors d'oeuvres
gambas prawns

judías beans
langosta spiny lobster
lechón/cochinillo suckling pig
mariscos shellfish
merluza hake
ostras oysters
pimiento bell pepper
pollo chicken
pulpo octopus
ternera veal
trucha trout
uvas grapes
verduras vegetables

Places to eat

The restaurant categories below reflect the cost of a three-course meal (starter, main course and dessert) plus a glass of house wine. At lunchtime, however, the majority of restaurants offer inexpensive two- or three-course fixed-priced menus (*menú del día* or *menú de la casa*), usually with two or three options for each course, making this, the main meal of the day, extremely affordable.

€€€€ = over 75 euros

€€€ = 40–75 euros

€€ = 25–40 euros

€ = below 25 euros

Plaza Mayor and La Latina

Botín Calle de Cuchilleros 17, www.botin.es. *Botín* claims to be world's oldest continuously running restaurant, having opened in 1725. Many clients are visitors to the city, but Spaniards are fans too. The nooks and crannies of the old dining rooms are appealing. The roast suckling pig and roast leg of lamb prepared in wood ovens give a great taste of traditional Castilian cooking. €€€

Casa Lucío Cava Baja 35, www.casalucio.es. A famous cave-like tavern, here since the 1970s, with hanging cured hams, popular with affluent locals and visitors alike. They serve high-quality Castilian cuisine: specialities include their legendary eggs with cured ham (*huevos estrellados*). €€€

Casa Paco Puerta Cerrada 11, www.casapaco1933.es. A classic eatery which has been here since the 1930s, serving up beef (priced by weight, seared and usually served very pink – a house speciality is beef cebón), grilled fish and, downstairs in the bar, cheese and cured ham. Attracts a stylish crowd. €€€

Julián de Tolosa Cava Baja 18, https://juliandetolosa.com. Superb plain Basque cooking: the huge charcoal-grilled rib steaks (*chuletón*) for two are a star dish, but the hake, black beans and red peppers are also good. Pricey, but a great dining experience. €€€€

Huertas, Santa Ana and Lavapiés

Casa Alberto Calle de las Huertas 18, www.casaalberto.es. An 1827-vintage tavern where Cervantes legendarily lived, this is a good place for *tapas* and beer pulled from an antique tap, or a sit-down meal. Meatballs, salt cod with red peppers and beef fillet are good choices. €€

Cerveceria Alemana Plaza Santa Ana 6, www.cerveceriaalemana.com. Whatever the service and food are like – both could be improved – this place is unmissable for some because of its connections with Hemingway. There's a good range of beers and an acceptable choice of homemade *tapas* and *raciones* (bigger portions). Food served until 2am at weekends. €€

La Musa de Espronceda Sta Isabel 17, www.lamuxadeespronceda.es. A short stroll from the Reina Sofía, this buzzy young bar-restaurant serves great set-lunches and creative Basque-style *tapas*, called *pintxos* (or *pinchos*, in Castilian Spanish) until past midnight to an arts crowd. Friday and Saturday evenings see up to fifty choices laid out on the bar. Excellent service. €€

Taberna La Alhambra Calle Victoria 9, tel: 91 521 0708. Decoratively tiled bar on a side street near Plaza Santa Ana. Established in 1929, it serves great Andalusian cooking, simple but well done. *Apéritivos* are free with drinks and the main dishes, from paella to fried goat's cheese, are good at fair prices. €

Palacio Real and Opera

La Bola Calle de la Bola 5, www.labola.es. This tiny, bright red restaurant on the corner of Calle de la Bola is a Madrid institution for its *cocido*, cooked in individual earthenware pots. Good shellfish and grilled meats and fish, too. Wonderful atmosphere. **€€**

Café de Oriente Plaza de Oriente 2, www.cafedeoriente.es. Staying open late, this brasserie is in a great location next to the Opera House, with summer terrace. Classic international cooking. Good for a late coffee or drink. **€€**

Taberna del Alabardero Calle Felipe V 4–6, www.alabarderomadrid.es. This classic tavern is a good place to visit after a night at the opera or for a rejuvenating lunch after touring the Palacio Real. It's a bustling *tapas* bar at the front and, at the back, a more select Basque restaurant serving fresh fish and exquisite meat dishes till midnight. **€€€**

Yerbabuena Calle de Bordadores 3, www.restaurante-yerbabuena. eatbu.com. Vegetarian restaurants can be hard to come by in Madrid but this is a good choice with an affordable but well-presented and highly diverse array of dishes. Spinach crêpes, aubergine burgers, fennel soup and mushroom pie are among the mains; to bring the price down even further, go for one of their set menus. **€**

Sol, Gran Via and Chueca

Artemisa Ventura de la Vega 4 and Tres Cruces 4, www.restaurantesve getarianosartemisa.com. A good, central vegetarian option, with two branches near the Prado and Gran Vía, serves creative dishes with very fresh ingredients. The lunch menu is very popular with nearby office workers. Rustic decor. Good wines, some organic. **€**

Las Bravas Calle de Álvarez Gato 3, www.lasbravas.com. Not exactly haute cuisine, but this simple (slightly cheesy-looking) spot specializes in *patatas bravas*, the king of Spanish comfort foods. They're served with a unique kind of sauce, and the venue itself has history, its novelty mirrors a hangover from the days when this was a barber's (and the subject of a story by Valle Inclán). €

Home Burger Calle de Silva 25, www.homeburgerbar.com. A small chain of organic burger bars offering simple gourmet variations like different cheese toppings, good wine and real chips. €

Lhardy Carrera de San Jerónimo 8, www.lhardy.com. Founded in 1839, *Lhardy* is part of Madrid's history, with formal nineteenth-century dining rooms upstairs and below a deli and *tapas* bar where you can enjoy pastries and consommé. The *cocido* is famous. €€€€

Paco Roncero Restaurante Calle Alcalá 15, www.pacoroncerorestaurante. com. Winner of multiple Michelin stars for avant-garde, yet personalized, cooking in the El Bullí school, which draws a stylish crowd to this grand dining room. Great wines and service. €€€€

La Pecera del Círculo de Bellas Artes Calle Alcalá 42, www.lapeceradel circulo.com. Think huge chandeliers, marble statues and vast windows with lovely views onto Alcalá. The set lunch is the best option at this restaurant-café, but there is a great atmosphere. Beautiful summer terrace. €€

Zara Calle Barbieri 8, www.restaurantezara.com. For something different, try this packed restaurant serving Cuban beans, stews and daiquiris in a genuine family atmosphere. You may need to queue (it's worth it). €€

Salamanca, Castellana and Prado

Café Gijón Paseo de Recoletos 21, www.cafegijon.com. Legendary literary café, fashionable with arty types since it opened in 1888. It still serves as a meeting place at any time of day, for a coffee or drink, lunch or supper. Set-price menus or à la carte. €€€

DiverXO Calle Padre Damian 23, Eurobuilding, www.diverxo.com. Consistently rated as one of Madrid's top avant-garde kitchens, producing tasting menus adapted to each table's tastes. The dozen or so dishes in each are beautiful to the eye and explore intriguing global flavours. Booking advised a month in advance. **€€€€**

Sagaretxe Calle Zurbano 43, www.sagaretxe.net. Set in a traditional cider house just west of Castellana, this place specializes in simple Basque food. If you like tortillas and pintxos, there's plenty to choose from here, as well as more filling meat and seafood mains. **€€**

Smoked Room Madrid Paseo de la Castellana, 57, www.grupodani garcia.com/lena. Madrid's most lauded hotel restaurant, a highly creative 'fire *omakase*' masterminded by star-chef Dani García. *Omakase* is, as you may be aware, a Japanese term essentially meaning 'chef's choice', and in Japanese fashion you'll be almost face-to-face with them; the 'fire' element here refers to the smoke produced while they're making most dishes. Good wines and service round out the picture. **€€€€**

Tragabuches Ortega y Gasset 40, www.grupodanigarcia.com/tragabuches. Another offering from the stable of Dani García, this time one showing off the cuisine of his home region of Andalucia. Pop by for breakfast, an 'Andalucia on your table' lunch, or dinner paired with some of Spain's best wine. **€€€€**

Outside Madrid

Ávila

El Molino de la Losa Bajada de la Losa 12, www.elmolinodelalosa.com. Enjoy great views from this ancient mill on an island in the middle of the River Adaja. Classic and modern cuisine. They also have a winery with an array of important regional wines. **€€€**

San Lorenzo El Escorial

Charolés Calle Floridablanca 24, www.charolesrestaurante.com. Inventive market cooking and a comprehensive wine list. Serves *cocido* on Wednesday and Friday, except for fiesta days. Luscious lemon and honey ice cream. €€€

Segovia

Mesón de Cándido Plaza Azoguejo 5, www.mesondecandido.es. This family-run restaurant in the shadow of the aqueduct has been an inn since the eighteenth century and was made a national monument in 1941. Legendary wood-roast meats. €€€

Restaurante del Cardenal Paseo Recaredo 24, www.haciendadelcardenal. com. The restaurant at the lovely *Hacienda del Cardenal* has long been one of Toledo's top kitchens. Best known for its wood roasts. Delightful summer terrace. €€€

Restaurante José María Cronista Lecea 11, www.restaurantejosemaria. com. A good stop whether you're just peckish or absolutely starving as there's a busy *tapas* bar at the front, as well as a relaxed restaurant. Try Segovian roasts or excellent Atlantic fish dishes. €€€

Toledo

Restaurante Adolfo Calle Hombre de Palo 7, www.adolforestaurante. com. Toledo haute cuisine is served in a medieval building near the cathedral. Game is a speciality here; the huge wine cellar is the city's finest. €€

Travel essentials

Practical information

Accessible travel

Madrid has certainly become easier to navigate over the last couple of decades. There are accessible rooms in many hotels and, by law, all new public buildings (including revamped museums and galleries) are required to be fully accessible; recent renovations of the Puerta del Sol and Plaza de España have made them far easier to navigate for everybody. Public transport is the main problem in Madrid, since boarding local buses and trains can prove a challenge for those in wheelchairs, though large parts of the metro network are accessible, and those heading out of the city will find that the AVE high-speed train services are fully accessible. Acoustic traffic-light signals and dropped kerbs are also common throughout Madrid.

Accommodation

Spanish hotels are rated by a star system, with five-star deluxe the top grade. The classifications often seem arbitrary; some two- and three-star places will be of the same quality as a hotel with a higher rating. Palatial and boutique hotels are clustered in the main tourist areas (Puerta del Sol, Gran Vía, Paseo del Prado and Chueca). About two-thirds of the city's hotels fall into the three- and four-star categories, while traditional *pensiones* (guesthouses) and *hostales* (modest, often family-owned hotels) are scattered around town. Breakfast (usually a continental-style buffet) is rarely included in the room rate.

I'd like a double/single room. **Me gustaría pedir una habitación doble/sencilla**
with/without bath/shower **con/sin baño/ducha**
double bed **cama matrimonial**
What's the rate per night? **¿Cuál es el precio por noche?**
Is breakfast included? **¿Está incluído el desayuno?**

Winter months (Nov–March) are formally the low season, but in practice prices often vary through the year, between weekends and weekdays, and according to booking levels. Madrid is very well represented on all of the major international booking sites and apps, though budget travellers may struggle to find something suitable at short notice.

Regulatory changes in 2024 mean that you now need to present ID and give your full home address when checking into any official accommodation in Spain, which has heaped extra (some would say unnecessary) work onto staff; many places will encourage you to check in online, which eases the burden somewhat.

Airport

Barajas Adolfo Suárez International Airport (MAD, www.aena.es), 12km (7.5 miles) northeast of Madrid, handles domestic and international flights. The airport has five terminals – T1, T2, T3, T4 and T4S, and note that if departing from the latter two, you might want to add on a little more time, since they can take a while to get to.

Taxis are available outside all terminals – allow 20–30 minutes to reach the city centre. One cheaper, equally reliable option is the 24-hour Autobús Express Aeropuerto (www.emtmadrid.es), which takes 30–40 minutes, with central drop-off and pick-up points at Plaza de Cibeles and Atocha railway station.

It's also easy to use Metro Line 8 from the airport to Nuevos Ministerios station, north of the city centre (journey time about 14min), from where Line 10 takes you to Plaza de España in about 15min. Annoyingly, you'll need to buy a transport card even for this one single journey, and to load it up and pay an airport supplement on the machines – if your destination is on or near the Renfe train network (very possible, since it's quite comprehensive), you can avoid both of these things by taking one of the regular trains from T4 to Chamartín (15min) station, and linking to other services there.

Apps

Firstly, yes, Uber works in Madrid, though many here prefer the local app, Cabify; Bolt is another alternative that you may already use. BiciMAD is the main local bike-sharing app, while Dott and Lime are two of several scooter versions. For maps, Google Maps works well here, as does offline alternative Maps.me, which has a Metro-system overlay that can assist with navigation.

Bicycle rental

Although Madrid has few cycle lanes, travelling by bicycle through the parks, pedestrianized streets and old quarter's quiet lanes is safe and pleasant, especially in good weather. Among various companies that offer bicycles for hire, Trixi (www.trixi.com) is very central and also offers tours and skateboards. For those who prefer bike-sharing apps for their ease of use, give BiciMAD a go; Dott and Lime are among the scooter options.

Budgeting for your trip

There are numerous ways to save money by planning ahead. Flight prices may be a quarter of the price midweek. Local transport services and the municipal, royal and regional tourist bodies make changing offers that are worth researching ahead of time. These include flat-price tickets for limitless metro and rail travel, and cut-price long-distance rail travel rates for advance booking. Buying the Paseo del Arte card gives you single entry to the three main museums of the city: the Prado, the Museo Reina Sofía and the Thyssen-Bornemisza. It saves around twenty percent versus buying the tickets separately, and is valid for one year.

By sticking to the excellent set-menus offered by bars and restaurants, you can keep your food expenses to a fixed budget. The Spanish breakfast of tomato on toast, with coffee, is widely available and almost always dirt cheap, even with *jamón* on top of the toast too, and a glass of freshly squeezed orange juice alongside – all a genuine pleasure, especially if it's sunny and you've managed to get a seat with a view. True budget travellers can also hunt down one of the many branches of *100 Montaditos* (www.100montaditos.com), which offers one hundred varieties of *montadito* (like miniature *bocadillos*) and other treats, plus beer and coffee, for super-low prices.

Camping

Madrid has an excellent year-round camping site a short metro or bus ride east of the city, at Alameda de Osuna. Camping Osuna, Jardines de Aranjuez 1, Metro Canillejas / El Capricho (www.campingosuna.com), rents spaces for tents and caravans. Facilities include a good bar-restaurant and small supermarket.

Car hire

To hire a car in Spain, you must usually be at least 21 years of age, with either an international driving licence or a valid licence (held at least for a year) from your own country. All motorcycle riders must wear helmets and ride with their headlights on, even during the day. Car hire must be paid for with a major credit card unless you leave a large deposit. Third-party insurance will be included; fully comprehensive may cost extra.

Cars can be hired per day with an additional fee according to mileage, or in package deals for a set number of days at unlimited mileage. Car hire agencies include:

Avis www.avis.es
Enterprise enterprise.es
Europcar www.europcar.es
Hertz www.hertz.es
Sixt www.sixt.es

Crime and safety

Though Madrid is no more dangerous than any other capital city, tourists should be on guard, especially close to the Prado (where scams are often perpetrated), the Rastro, Gran Vía, Puerta del Sol, Plaza Mayor, Plaza de Toros bullring, on the Metro or at any large street gathering. The most common crimes are pickpocketing and the snatching of passports and handbags.

As ever, it pays to be careful. Do not leave luggage unattended; don't carry more money on your person than you'll need for daily expenses; use the hotel safe deposit for larger sums and valuables; in crowds around street attractions and sports events, be on your guard against pickpockets;

reject offers of flowers or other objects from street pedlars – they may be after your wallet; don't leave valuables in view inside your car, even when it's locked; photocopy personal documents and leave the originals in your hotel.

If you are robbed, contact the local police station, or dial 092 for the city police (*policía municipal*).

I want to report a theft. **Quiero denunciar un robo**
My ticket/wallet/passport/purse has been stolen. **Me han robado mi billete/cartera/pasaporte/monadera**

Driving

Crossing the border into Spain, you won't be asked for documents, but in the event of any problem you will have to produce your passport, driving licence, registration papers and insurance documents, which must be carried with you at all times when driving.

Cruce peligroso Dangerous crossroads
Curva peligrosa Dangerous bend
Despacio Slow
Peligro Danger
Prohibido adelantar No overtaking (passing)
Prohibido aparcar No parking
Sentido único One way (street)

It's best to avoid driving in Madrid. Nerve-wracking traffic jams are a way of life, although there is a lull between 3 and 4.30pm. There are many accidents on the streets in the early hours of the morning, when the clubs close.

Rules and regulations: You should display a nationality sticker on your car. Most fines for traffic offences are payable on the spot or at a bank within a set time limit. Driving rules are the same throughout Spain: drive on the right, overtake (pass) on the left, yield right of way to vehicles coming from the right (unless your road is marked as having priority). Front and rear seat belts are compulsory.

Speed limits are 120kmh (75mph) on motorways, 100kmh (62mph) on broad main roads (two lanes each way), 90kmh (56mph) on other main roads, 50kmh (31mph), or as marked, in densely populated areas.

If you need help: Garages are efficient, but repairs may take time in busy areas. In an emergency, tel: 091.

Electricity

The standard electric current is 220 volts, but some hotels have a voltage of 110–120 in bathrooms as a safety precaution. Check before plugging in any appliance. Sockets (outlets) take round, two-pin plugs, so you will probably need an international adapter plug.

Embassies and consulates

Many Western European countries have embassies in Madrid. Some useful addresses are as follows:

Australia: Torre Espacio, Paseo de la Castellana 259d, tel: 91 353 6600; www.spain.embassy.gov.au.

Canada: Torre Espacio, Paseo de la Castellana 259d, tel: 91 382 8400; www. international.gc.ca.

Ireland: Paseo de la Castellana 46, tel: 91 436 4093; www.ireland.ie.

New Zealand: Calle del Pinar 7, 3rd floor, tel: 91 523 0226; www.mfat.govt.nz.

UK: Torre Espacio, Paseo de la Castellana 259d, tel: 91 714 6300; www.gov. uk (NB: Citizens of Commonwealth countries may apply to the UK embassy).

United States: Calle de Serrano 75, tel: 91 587 2200; https://es.usembassy. gov.

Emergencies

In the event of an emergency, contact the relevant source of assistance:

Coordinated Emergency Number: 112
Emergency Medical Care: 112
Ambulance: 061 or 901 222 222 (Red Cross/Cruz Roja)
City Police: 092
National Police: 091
Guardia Civil: 062
Fire Service (Madrid): 080

Getting there

By air

Madrid's airport Barajas is linked by daily non-stop flights from across Europe. Most flights from the US and Canada are direct; others stop first in Lisbon, Frankfurt or London. From Australia and New Zealand, regular one-stop flights go directly to Madrid.

There are direct flights to Madrid from the UK via British Airways (www.ba.com) and Iberia (www.iberia.es), as well as low-cost Vueling (www.vueling.com), easyJet (www.easyjet.com) and Ryanair (www.ryanair.com) flights from various airports. There are services between Madrid and the United States with Iberia, Delta and American Airlines (www.aa.com).

Domestic services are operated by Iberia, Vueling, Ryanair and others.

By road

The main access road from France to Madrid skirts the western end of the Pyrenees. A motorway (expressway) runs from Biarritz (France) through the Basque Country via Bilbao to Burgos, from where you take the E25 motorway straight down to Madrid, 240km (150 miles) away.

Express coach services operate between London and Madrid, as well as between other European cities and Madrid. For further details, visit www.flixbus.com or www.eurolines.eu.

By rail

Anyone travelling from the UK should take the Eurostar to Paris, from where there are overnight trains to Madrid. For discounts and special rail tickets, see page 138.

Guides and tours

The Centro de Turismo de Madrid (City Tourism Office, Plaza Mayor 27, daily 9.30am–9.30pm; www.esmadrid.com) offers personal advice, and historical and cultural tours by bus and on foot throughout the year, covering a wide array of topics and sights. Madrid City Tour (https://madrid.city-tour.com) organizes hop-on, hop-off multi-language city bus tours that depart from the Prado several times daily.

Health and medical care

Standards of hygiene are high, and medical care in Madrid is excellent. Most doctors speak sufficient English to deal with foreign patients. The water is safe to drink, but bottled water is always safest, and is available everywhere. Most local people drink bottled water, *agua con gas* (carbonated) or *sin gas* (still). It is good, clean and inexpensive.

Visitors from EU countries with corresponding health-insurance facilities are entitled to medical and hospital treatment under the Spanish social security system. You must have your European Health Insurance Card (EHIC) card with you for reciprocal health care – any British nationals that still have one of these will probably notice that it's out of date, and will need their Global Health Insurance Card (GHIC).

It is recommended that you also take out reputable private medical insurance, which will be part of almost all travel insurance packages.

Chemists (*farmacias*) operate as a first line of defence for Spaniards, as pharmacists can prescribe drugs and are usually adept at making on-the-spot diagnoses. Pharmacies, marked by a green neon cross lit up when open, operate during normal business hours and one in every district remains open all night and on holidays. The location and phone number of this *farmacia de guardia* is posted on the door of all the other pharmacies. All-night pharmacies can also be contacted by calling 098. To locate a hospital or report a medical emergency, dial 112.

If you take drugs on prescription, ensure that you take extra supplies with you. Spanish chemists do not honour foreign prescriptions. Given the dry climate and sun levels, it is a good idea to wear sunscreen and carry water with you in both summer and winter.

Language

After Chinese and English, the most widely spoken language in the world is Spanish, from Madrid to Manila, from Ávila to Argentina. The Castilian spoken in Madrid is understood in most areas of Spain. It's certainly worth learning a few basic phrases; though many locals speak English, the general level isn't as high as in most of Western Europe.

LGBTQ+ travellers

Madrid has a vibrant LGBTQ+ scene, which is centred in the neighbourhood of Chueca, whose grid of narrow lanes lies just north of the Gran Vía. The local multitude of bars and clubs vary from low-key to hardcore, and magazines on LGBTQ+ social life, such as *Shangay* (https://shangay.com), give further information. This *barrio's* small café-lined central square is a hive of hetero-LGBTQ+ activity during the summer and is a good place to meet people.

Gay Pride week, at the end of June, includes a high-heels race and a Saturday procession with floats that is a hugely popular fiesta with young and old alike, bringing the city centre to a standstill.

Money

The currency of Spain is the euro, which comes in coins valued 1 euro, 2 euros, plus 50, 20, 10, 5, 2 and 1 cents. Bills are in denominations of 5, 10, 20, 50, 100, 200 and 500 euros.

Credit and debit cards

These are used extensively in Spain, and most towns have cashpoint facilities, which are generally the cheapest way to get your hands on some cash.

> Where's the nearest bank/currency exchange office?**¿Dónde está el banco/la casa de cambio más cercana?**
> I want to change some pounds/dollars. **Quiero cambiar libras/dólares.**
> Can I pay with a credit card? **¿Se puede pagar con tarjeta?**
> How much is that? **¿Cuánto es?**

Opening times

The practice of the siesta – the long midday break and nap – is losing adherents in Madrid, except in the hot months. The big department stores and supermarkets remain open all day, as do many shops, though for smaller shops the usual hours are from 9.30am–1.30pm or 2pm, and 5pm–8pm, Mon–Sat. Some shops close on Saturday afternoons. Increasingly, department stores and high street chain outlets open on Sundays. Major museums have generally shifted to unbroken day-long opening.

Restaurants serve lunch from 1pm–4pm; in the evening their timing depends on the kind of customers they expect. Local people usually eat between 9 and 11pm or later. Places catering to foreigners may function from 7pm on, and many stay open throughout the day.

Banks are usually open Mon–Fri 9am–2pm. Some banks such as La Caixa open on Thursday evening. All banks close on Saturday afternoon, Sunday and fiestas.

Police

Spanish municipal and national police are efficient, strict and courteous – and generally very responsive to issues involving foreign tourists. In Madrid, dial 092 for municipal police and 091 for national police. The central police station (Policía Nacional), with interpreters, is located at Calle Leganitos 19, near Plaza de España (www.policia.es; tel: 91 322 4097).

Public holidays

January 1 *Año Nuevo* (New Year's Day)

January 6 *Epifanía* (Epiphany)

January 20 *San Sebastián* (St Sebastian's Day)

May 1 *Fiesta del Trabajo* (Labour Day)

July 25 *Santiago Apóstol* (St James's Day)

August 15 *Asunción* (Assumption)

October 12 *Día de la Hispanidad* (Discovery of America Day/Spanish National Day)

November 1 *Todos los Santos* (All Saints' Day)

December 6 *Día de la Constitución* (Constitution Day)

December 8 *Inmaculada Concepción* (Immaculate Conception)

December 25 *Navidad* (Christmas Day)

December 26 *La Fiesta Navidad* (Christmas holiday)

Moveable dates

Jueves Santo (Holy Thursday)

Viernes Santo (Good Friday)

Lunes de Pascua (Easter Monday)

Corpus Christi (Corpus Christi)

In addition to these nationwide holidays, there are big celebrations in Madrid on **May 2** (*El Dos de Mayo*), and public holidays on **May 15**, the city's patron saint's day (*San Isidro Labrador*/St Isidore the Husbandman), and on **November 9** (*La Almudena*).

Telephones

Spain's country code is 34 and Madrid's local area 91.

Mobile phone use in EU countries is included in most monthly plans, but some restrictions and exceptions still apply. If in doubt, contact your local provider for more information before you travel.

The main international mobile operators in Spain are Vodafone, Orange and Yoigo. The main Spanish operator is Movistar.

Time zones

Spanish time coincides with the rest of Western Europe – Greenwich Mean

Time plus one hour. In spring, another hour is added for Daylight Saving Time (Summer Time).

Tipping

Service is usually included in restaurant bills, but it is customary to leave the spare change in the dish when eating at a modest restaurant and a few cents at a bar. When dining at a fairly smart restaurant, an additional 5–10 percent of the bill is appropriate. Small change or a 10 percent tip is fine for an average taxi ride.

Toilets

Toilet doors are distinguished by a 'C' for *Caballeros* (gentlemen) or 'S' for *Señoras* (ladies) or by a variety of pictographs (often amusing).

> **Where are the toilets? ¿Dónde están los servicios?**

Tourist information

The national (www.spain.info) and city (www.esmadrid.com) tourist sites have plenty of useful information.

Tourist information for Madrid, and indeed all of Spain, is available at the tourist offices (*oficinas de información turística*) in Barajas airport (T1 and T4 arrivals), at Duque de Medinaceli 2, in Chamartín station, and in Atocha station. All open Mon–Fri 8 or 9am–7 or 8pm, Sat 9am–1 or 2pm.

The main Madrid city tourist office is at Plaza Mayor 27 (Casa de Panadería), tel: 91-578 7810, and is open daily 9.30am–9.30pm. There are information kiosks dotted elsewhere around town.

For telephone information on tourist facilities and practical matters, tel: 010 for the City Information Office.

Transport

Madrid has a reliable and comprehensive public transport system. Getting around town, especially by Metro (subway/tube) is easy, rapid, and inexpensive, though for Metro rides you'll need to buy a transport card. One website provides information for all services: www.crtm.es.

Buses (autobuses)

Inner-city buses currently operate a set fare regardless of the route or length of journey in the city centre. You enter from the front and pay the driver (card or cash) or stamp your multi-journey ticket. You don't need to have the exact fare, but you should offer coins, or €5 notes at most. Press the buzzer at the stop you require and leave by the rear door.

An *Abono* is good for ten journeys by bus or Metro and works out much cheaper than buying ten individual tickets. It can be purchased from the bus information booths at Puerta del Sol, Plaza Callao, Plaza de la Cibeles and Plaza de Castilla, as well as in every Metro station.

If you are planning to spend an extended period of time in Madrid and doing a lot of bus and Metro travelling, purchase an *Abono 30 días*. This card can be applied for at any *estanco* by filling out a form and providing a passport-size photograph and a photocopy of your passport or national identity document. It is valid for a month, with reductions for people under 18 and over 65.

Buses are in service 6am–11.30pm.

Metro

The Madrid Metro system is the fastest, cheapest and most efficient way of getting around the city. It operates from 6am–1.30am. Most trains have air-conditioning. Central journeys have flat rates, and you can buy a cut-rate *Abono*, which allows you to make ten trips (by Metro or bus) or a 1-, 2-, 3-, 5- or 7-day *Abono Turístico*. You will need to purchase a transport card to ride the Metro; this is easy to do at the ticket machines.

Taxis

Madrid taxis are relatively inexpensive, and can be hailed with relative ease on main thoroughfares or found at *paradas de taxi* (taxi stands). They are available if they are displaying a green *libre* (free) sign on the windscreen or

have a little green light on. If a red sign with the name of a Madrid neighbourhood is displayed, it means it is on its way home and not obliged to
pick you up unless you are going in the same direction. A meter on the
dashboard indicates an initial fare at the start of the journey, and chalks up
an extra sum for every kilometre.

Ride-hailing apps are widely used in Madrid; see page 126 for some tips.

Trains (trenes)

The national rail system (www.renfe.com) has a suburban network that
almost acts as a second metro system; timetables for these trains rarely
come up on the main Renfe website, but Google Maps tends to be accurate in this regard when planning journeys.

If leaving the city, Madrid's northern railway station, **Chamartín**, handles AVE and regular services to Segovia and beyond, as well as some services to the country's east. **Atocha** station, in the south of the city, operates
AVE and other services to and from destinations to the south, east and
west, including Toledo, Barcelona and Valencia.

When's the next train to…? **¿Cuándo sale el próximo tren
   para…?**
A ticket to… **Un billete para…**
single (one-way) **ida**
return (round-trip) **ida y vuelta**
What's the fare to…? **¿Cuánto es la tarifa a …?**

Visas and entry requirements

Visitors from the EU (and citizens of Andorra, Liechtenstein, Monaco and
Switzerland) require only a valid national identity card from their home
state to enter Spain. As British citizens have no identity cards, they need a
passport, and are subject to a maximum of ninety days in the Schengen
zone in any 180-day period; the same advice goes for citizens of the United
States, Australia and New Zealand, as well the non-Schengen parts of Eu-

rope, and most of South America. Visitors from elsewhere must obtain a visa from the Spanish consulate in their own country before setting off. Passport or identity card numbers are often required with flight bookings as a security measure.

In order to reside in Spain for an extended period, a Residencia (*Visado de Residencia Serie V*) must be obtained from the Spanish embassy or consulate in one's country of origin. EU nationals are allowed to live and work in Spain, but should check residency requirements with their nearest Spanish embassy before departure.

Websites

www.tourspain.es Site of Turespaña, the National Tourism Office.
www.esmadrid.com Madrid City Council's website, with links to transport and accommodation information.
www.patrimonionacional.es Website for numerous monuments, museums, parks and other sights owned by the Spanish royal family.

Index

RED DE METRO Y METRO LIGERO *Metro and Light Rail Network*

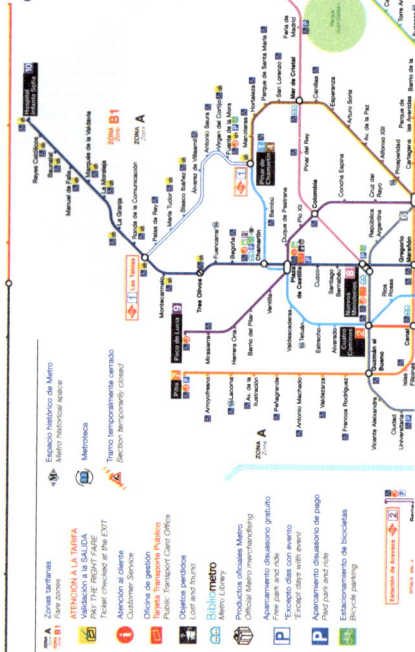

Metro de Madrid – Plano de la red

MINI
MADRID

First Edition 2025

Editor: Libby Davies
Author: Martin Zatko
Picture Manager: Tom Smyth
Cartography Update: Katie Bennett
Layout: Danielle Titmas
Production Operations Manager: Katie Bennett
Publishing Technology Manager: Rebeka Davies
Head of Publishing: Sarah Clark
Photography Credits: Bigstock 36; Carlos Delgado 20CL; Corrie Wingate/Apa Publications 14TL, 14CL, 41, 46, 79, 102; Dreamstime 70, 73; Grupo Dani Garcia 18CL; iStock 7, 11, 15CT, 16CL, 16BR, 35, 38, 39, 42, 45, 47, 48, 60, 62, 69, 81, 83, 90, 94, 114; Museo Nacional del Prado 56; Public domain 14CR, 22, 25, 26, 28, 52, 53; Robert B. Fishman/Picfair 50; Shutterstock 1, 8, 13, 14BL, 14TR, 14BR, 15T, 15CB, 15B, 16T, 16BL, 18T, 18BL, 18BR, 20T, 20BL, 20BR, 31, 32, 34, 51, 55, 57, 58, 60, 64, 65, 67, 74, 76, 77, 80, 84, 86, 88, 89, 92, 97, 98, 101, 103, 105, 106, 108, 110, 113, 116
Cover Credits: King Philip III Statue in Plaza Mayor **iStock**

About the author

Martin Zatko has written or contributed to almost fifty Insight Guides and Rough Guides since making his debut in 2006, including those to Korea, Japan, China, Vietnam, Myanmar, Malaysia, India, Turkey, Greece, Morocco, Australia, Fiji and Egypt.

Distribution

UK, Ireland and Europe: Apa Publications (UK) Ltd; mail@roughguides.com
United States and Canada: Two Rivers; ips@ingramcontent.com
Australia and New Zealand: Woodslane; info@woodslane.com.au
Worldwide: Apa Publications (UK) Ltd; mail@roughguides.com

MIX
Paper | Supporting responsible forestry
FSC
www.fsc.org
FSC® C106499

Special Sales, Content Licensing and CoPublishing

Rough Guides can be purchased in bulk quantities at discounted prices. We can create special editions, personalized jackets and corporate imprints tailored to your needs.
mail@roughguides.com
roughguides.com

EU Representative

LOGOS EUROPE, 9 rue Nicolas Poussin, 17000, LA ROCHELLE, France; Contact@logoseurope.eu; +33 (0) 667937378

Printed by Omur in Turkey

ISBN: 9781835294918

This book was produced using **Typefi** automated publishing software.

A catalogue record for this book is available from the British Library

All Rights Reserved
© 2025 Apa Digital AG
License edition © Apa Publications Ltd UK

No part of this book may be reproduced, stored in a retrieval system, or transmitted in any form or by any means – electronic, mechanical, photocopying, recording, or otherwise – without prior written permission from Apa Publications.

No part of this book may be used or reproduced in any manner for the purpose of training artificial intelligence technologies or systems.

Contact us

Every effort has been made to ensure that this publication is accurate, free from safety risks, and provides accurate information. However, changes and errors are inevitable. The publisher is not responsible for any resulting loss, inconvenience, injury or safety concerns arising from the use of this book. If you notice any errors, outdated information, or potential safety risks, please send your comments with the subject line "Rough Guide Mini Book Title Update" to mail@roughguides.com.